S0-AIP-821

Tell Me Your Names and I Will Testify

TELL ME YOUR NAMES AND I WILL TESTIFY

Carolyn Holbrook

University of Minnesota Press

Minneapolis | London

Excerpts from "Yellow Taxi" by Eve Joseph, from *At the End of Life: True Stories about How We Die,* Lee Gutkind, editor (Creative Nonfiction Books, 2012), are reprinted with permission of the author.

Excerpts from *Sisters of the Yam: Black Women and Self-Recovery* by bell hooks (Boston: South End Press, 1994) are reprinted with permission of the author.

Lines from Lucille Clifton, "at the cemetery, walnut grove plantation, south carolina, 1989" from *The Collected Poems of Lucille Clifton.* Copyright 1991 by Lucille Clifton. Reprinted with permission of The Permissions Company, LLC, on behalf of BOA Editions Ltd., www.boaeditions.org.

Lines from "Ego-Tripping (there must be a reason why)" from *The Collected Poetry of Nikki Giovanni, 1968–1998* by Nikki Giovanni. Copyright for compilation 2003 by Nikki Giovanni. Reprinted by permission of HarperCollins Publishers.

Copyright 2020 by Carolyn Lee Holbrook

All rights reserved. No part of this publication may be reproduced, stored in a retrieval system, or transmitted, in any form or by any means, electronic, mechanical, photocopying, recording, or otherwise, without the prior written permission of the publisher.

Published by the University of Minnesota Press
111 Third Avenue South, Suite 290
Minneapolis, MN 55401-2520
http://www.upress.umn.edu

Printed in Canada on acid-free paper

The University of Minnesota is an equal-opportunity educator and employer.

25 24 23 22 21 20   10 9 8 7 6 5 4 3 2 1

LIBRARY OF CONGRESS CATALOGING-IN-PUBLICATION DATA

Holbrook, Carolyn (Carolyn L.), author.

Tell me your names and I will testify / Carolyn Holbrook.

Minneapolis : University of Minnesota Press, 2020.

Identifiers: LCCN 2019036805 (print) | ISBN 978-1-5179-0763-1 (pb)

Subjects: LCSH: Holbrook, Carolyn (Carolyn L.) | African American women authors—21st century—Biography. | African American women authors—Political and social views.

Classification: LCC PS3608.O482875 Z46 2020 (print) | DDC 818/.603 [B]—dc23

LC record available at https://lccn.loc.gov/2019036805

To Mom and Barney
and to my ancestral mothers,
on whose shoulders I stand

nobody mentioned slaves
and yet the curious tools
shine with your fingerprints.
nobody mentioned slaves
but somebody did this work
who had no guide, no stone,
who moulders under rock.

tell me your names.
tell me your bashful names
and I will testify.

—Lucille Clifton, from "at the cemetery,
walnut grove plantation,
south carolina, 1989"

CONTENTS

PROLOGUE Liza / *1*

1 My Roots / *7*

2 Coming Clean / *11*

3 Tania's Birthday / *27*

4 The "Award" / *47*

5 Finally Independent / *63*

6 Reflections on Teaching / *75*

7 Expectations and Assumptions / *83*

8 How Long Does It Take? / *99*

9 I Want to Know My Name / *105*

10 The Bank Robbery / *111*

11 Neighborhood Watch / *123*

12 My Daughter, Myself / *127*

13 Sex and the Single Grandma / *137*

14 Say What? / *147*

15 Earth Angels / *159*

16 Stones and Sticks / *179*

ACKNOWLEDGMENTS / *185*

PUBLICATION HISTORY / *187*

Prologue

LIZA

We go on with the dead inside us.

—Eve Joseph, "Yellow Taxi"

Two years before I celebrated my fiftieth birthday I moved into my parents' duplex in South Minneapolis. Not because they needed me; my stepfather had passed away some years before, and Mom, a petite but tough and feisty lady in her seventies, was as strong as she had ever been. The move was the result of some unexpected financial problems that occurred after I resigned from an untenable employment situation and was struck with a serious illness before I could find a new job. My severance—including my medical benefits—had dried up. My home was about to be foreclosed on and my savings account was quickly dwindling.

My youngest daughter, sixteen-year-old Ebony, was the last of my five children still living at home. It was important to me that she continue to have a stable environment, but it was humiliating to be returning to my childhood home at an age when I should have been creating a comfortable space for my grandchildren. Nevertheless, I couldn't deny my good fortune. My parents' long-term tenants had purchased a home of their own and were moving out at the same time I had to vacate my house.

My parents' duplex, built in 1935 in a quiet neighborhood near Minnehaha Creek, was beautiful and spacious. A large picture window invited the sun into the living room during the day and enticed the moon and stars to cast mysterious shadows at night. Hardwood floors that shone like honey stretched from the living and dining rooms all the way through to the three bedrooms, each as big as some of my friends' apartments, and a cozy breakfast nook nestled in a corner of the roomy kitchen.

One evening a couple of months after we were settled in, I kissed my daughter goodbye and sent her off to whatever teenage thing she was doing that autumn night. It had been a long day of meetings for a new literary arts organization I was in the process of building, and I was looking forward to a night of solitude. I slid a movie into the VHS player and slumped down on the sofa and was about to dig into a bowl of freshly popped popcorn when I thought I saw something shadowy out of the corner of my eye. I didn't pay much attention, thinking it was probably my long-deceased maternal grandfather who had been making periodic visits since my difficult pregnancy with Ebony—always showing up in the wheelchair he smiled from in a sepia-toned photograph that has held a prominent place in my mother's home for as long as I can remember.

Feeling comforted that Grandfather Robert had stopped by to check on me once again, I turned back to my popcorn and *Sleepless in Seattle,* which was about to begin. Soon an odd, icy breeze passed through the room. I looked toward the door wondering if I had left it open a crack and was taken aback to see a tall, stately woman standing there. She was dressed in a Victorian-era gown made of an expensive silken fabric woven in wide, vertical black-and-antique-gold stripes. Dainty buttons, covered in the same fabric, snaked up the bodice from her waist to her neck where a neckband, topped with fine lace, encircled her throat. A bustled skirt drifted from her tiny waist to the floor and long sleeves, puffed at the shoulders, hid her graceful arms. A large hat, enhanced with what appeared to be ostrich plumes, covered her black pompadour. She was accompanied by a tall, dapper gentleman dressed in a tan suit and a top hat, and his arm was looped possessively through hers. I stared in disbelief, almost dropping my popcorn.

I was stunned by this ghostly intrusion, yet I somehow knew she was a relative, an ancestor. Fear and curiosity flooded over me as I wondered who she was and why she was there. She gazed at me with intense, dark eyes and then, as though responding to my thoughts, said, "I am Liza. You have to tell our story." And just like that, she and her gentleman were gone.

Visits from loved ones who have passed on were not new to me. Just the year before, my sister called on me to help her decide whether to stay on the Earth plane or to cross over after she had suffered a brain aneurysm. Though she was in San Francisco and I was in Minneapolis, I reached through the veil and held her hand, and I knew the moment the aneurysm took her life. Also, my beloved stepfather paid me a reassuring visit when I woke up from surgery shortly after he passed away in 1984. And, of course, there was Grandfather Robert. But this was the first time a spirit showed up with an explicit command.

Once I recovered and could breathe again, my mind was full of questions. Why was I the one she came to? What does she want me to say? What parts of my family's story want to be told, need to be told? Which will demand to be told? Who will be hurt by what I write? Who will be healed?

IT WAS IMPOSSIBLE to sleep that night, so when Ebony got home—a few minutes past her curfew—I told her what had happened. All three of my daughters are used to hearing my stories of ghostly visitations, but a visit from a spirit with an explicit command was new to all of us. Ebony had questions that mirrored mine. So did my two older daughters, Iris and Tania, when I told them the next day.

I knew I had no choice but to follow Liza's command, but I didn't have a clue where to begin. I thought that maybe my first step should be to try and find out who she was. The next day I asked my mother if she knew of someone from our past named Liza. I was reluctant to share the reason for my question, fearing that she wouldn't believe me or would ridicule me for what she tended to characterize as my overactive imagination. Thankfully, she didn't ask, choosing only to tell me that she didn't know of anyone by that name.

I then called my cousin Stephanie and my step-mother, Joyce, both genealogists. Joyce said she had found a Liza in my father's ancestry, but all she could give me was the name; she didn't know her story.

Cousin Stephanie, on the other hand, who also receives occasional visitations, said she had uncovered an Eliza in her research of my matrilineal line: an enslaved woman who was living at the same time as the Liza my stepmother had found. Eliza had lived on the plantation of a slave owner named John Lee and gave birth to my mixed-race Grandfather Robert, giving him the surname Lee. She moved to Denver, Colorado, with her son in the Gold Rush era.

It is unclear whether Eliza escaped after enduring sexual exploitation or if, perhaps, she was John Lee's mistress. From what we know of chattel slavery, either story could have been true. It is no secret that many of our foremothers were raped at random—often repeatedly by the same man, and then bore his children. We also know that slaves were sold at the whim of the "owner" whose "property" they were. But there are also stories of slave women and children who were taken care of by men who loved them.

Based on some of what I know about the history of my people, of my family's history, and also of my own life, I started writing whatever came into my mind, mostly drivel. After a while, stories began to form. Most writers are familiar with the muse who helps us with our writing and the internal critic who tries to put roadblocks in our path. For me, the muse and the critic are the voices of my maternal aunts, both who have been in the ancestral realm for many years. Sometimes when I'm working on a difficult passage, I imagine them sitting on my shoulders: the aunt who held strong religious beliefs sits on my left shoulder shaking her finger and saying, "Now don't you go stirring things up." My other aunt sits on my right shoulder, a cigarette in one hand and a glass of scotch in the other. She smiles encouragingly and says, "Don't hold back, child. Someone out there needs to hear what you have to say." Sometimes it is difficult to find the balance between their words and mine, what to say and what to leave out. I do the best I can.

WE LOST MOTHER in 2013. In her will, she stated that she wanted me to sell the duplex and split the proceeds between myself, my stepbrother, and my niece. I moved back into her home once again, having decided to spend a year clearing things out and preparing the house to sell. Mom and Barney had lived there some forty years, and clearing it out would be a difficult task. But with my children and grandchildren's help, I managed to get it done.

One day while going through family photographs I gasped upon coming across an old sepia photograph that I had never seen before, a picture of a woman who resembled the woman who had stood at my door that night so long ago and identified herself as Liza. Tall and stately, she was dressed just as I had seen her that night in 1993: in a Victorian-era gown made of an expensive silken fabric woven in wide, vertical black and antique gold stripes. Dainty buttons covered in the same fabric snaked up the bodice from her waist to her neck where a neckband topped with fine lace encircled her throat. A bustled skirt drifted from her tiny waist to the floor and long sleeves, puffed at the shoulders, hid her graceful arms. A large hat, enhanced with ostrich plumes, covered her thick, black pompadour. Her piercing eyes gazed out at me from the picture frame the same way they bored into me that night in 1993, as though reiterating her command.

The stories of trauma that started with the enslavement of my people in 1619 when the first known slave ship, the *Man of War*, docked in Jamestown, Virginia—coupled with the traumas that we continue to endure today—make it clear that we need to keep telling our stories, that the healing power of story cannot be stressed enough. This is what Liza demanded.

1

MY ROOTS

Let's leave tonight promising to tell our stories,
because we weren't intended to survive.

—Dr. Josie R. Johnson on the evening of the
launch of her memoir, *Hope in the Struggle*

I was a small child when my parents divorced. My mother moved my three siblings and me from our home in Ann Arbor, Michigan, to make a new life in Minneapolis, and Dad moved his new family to Springfield, Massachusetts.

Life is never easy for a single parent, and Mama was no exception. I always bristle when I hear white feminists talk about work as a privilege. Black women have always had to work, often cleaning the houses of wealthy white women who were "privileged" to work outside their homes. In addition to cleaning houses, Mama also did piecework in a factory where she was paid according to the amount of work she produced. But even with two jobs, she had to resort to commodities such as government cheese and a spam-like meat substance in order to keep food on the table. Even so, she kept our home spotless, made our clothes, kept us clean, and nursed us through our childhood illnesses. She found creative ways to stretch that tasteless government food, often inventing dishes she hoped we would enjoy, being sure to include healthy servings of fruit and the fresh vegetables she grew in the garden she kept on the side of our house. And she spent a lot of time in the hot summers canning so the produce from her garden would last through the cold Minnesota winter months.

Like her mother before her, my mother wanted to be a hairstylist. Over time, she accomplished her dream in a much larger way than she envisioned when she was a young mother struggling to keep food on the table. She worked her way through beauty school and then went to work at Bea's Beauty Shop in South Minneapolis. Her struggle continued for a while, but things got easier after she met Barney. I was about twelve years old when Mama and Barney married and he brought his young son to live with us. A gentle and loving man, Barney was a terrific father and stepfather. He adored my mother and us children. Mama treated his son as though he were her own child, and we all accepted him as our brother. To this day, my children's faces brighten during frequent mentions of Grandpa Barney.

In his professional life, Welton "Barney" Barnett was the first Black auditor for the Minnesota Department of Agriculture. But his real passion was music. He picked his left-landed Fender Telecaster guitar in small combos and also with a big band that played in a ritzy suburban supper club called the White House. We kids loved watching him when he sat on the couch quietly practicing, his amplifier turned off so as not to disturb the family, and we enjoyed dancing around in time to the music when his friends came over to practice in our basement. It was unfortunate that in keeping with the times Barney was forced to enter the supper club through the back door while his white bandmates went in through the front door. While I was preparing for an estate sale after Mama and Barney passed away, I came across an obituary about Barney in an archived 1985 edition of *Downbeat Magazine.* There, for the first time, we children learned that he had played with jazz legends Cab Calloway and Duke Ellington "in his NYC heydays in the '40s."

Mama and Barney both had good heads for business, and together they opened Mama's own beauty salon, Jo-anna Salon of Beauty on Forty-eighth Street and Fourth Avenue in South Minneapolis at a time when the practice of redlining limited Black families to living and doing business in areas that were not as far south as that neighborhood.

Later, after her first employer, Bea, passed away, they bought the building Bea had owned and turned it into a beauty school. Career Beauty Academy was the first and only African American beauty school to ever exist in the State of Minnesota. Unfortunately, they were unable to sustain it. It closed after five short years. But that did not stop my courageous mother. She opened another salon and also accepted an invitation to start a Cosmetology program in the Minneapolis Public Schools, a program that still exists at Edison High School. And when she was almost sixty years old, after she had owned and operated two beauty salons and the beauty school, and after she had started the program for the public schools, I proudly witnessed my amazing mother march across the stage of Northrop Auditorium at the University of Minnesota to accept the bachelor of science degree in vocational education she had earned.

I come from a long line of role models, Black women entrepreneurs and educators. My maternal grandmother developed and sold a line of hair products and taught her patrons how to use them. My great-grandmother, together with my great-grandfather, turned their home into a boarding house for African American railroad porters in Lincoln, Nebraska, where porters were not allowed to stay in hotels. I am proud to be the inheritor of my foremothers' remarkable, enterprising spirit. It is because of their legacy that I have been able to achieve as much as I have.

2

COMING CLEAN

Words are to be taken seriously. I try to take seriously acts of language. Words set things in motion. I've seen them doing it. Words set up atmospheres, electrical fields, charges. I've felt them doing it. Words conjure.

—Toni Cade Bambara

On one of the many days that I stood at the front desk in the Minneapolis South High School office signing in my tardy daughter, the assistant principal asked me to come into her office. I braced myself, expecting to be warned of possible consequences for Ebony's habitual lateness. But instead Ms. Rudel said she had been observing my relationship with my daughter, which she characterized as close, loving, and "beautiful." She said there were many other African American girls at South who could benefit from having a mother figure like me in their lives, then asked if I would consider taking one or two of them under my wing.

Relieved and surprised, I was pleased that the way I relate to my children had caught Ms. Rudel's scrutinizing eye. But there were things about our circumstances that she was not aware of. Ebony was just beginning to recover from a struggle that had begun two years earlier when Tania, my middle daughter and her closest sibling, left home for college. In some ways Tania had been the mother figure to Ebony that Ms. Rudel hoped I could be to one of the young women she had in mind.

She didn't know that when Ebony was in middle school and Tania was in her junior year of high school, I had accepted a full-time position working outside our home. This was new for Ebony, because until then I had been working at home her entire life.

Tania and Ebony were the last of my five children still at home, and they spent a good two years together after school doing homework and watching *After School Specials* on television until I got home from work every day. But Tania was accepted to a prestigious college in New York during her senior year. While our family was proud of her and very excited, Tania's good fortune was devastating for Ebony. All of her older siblings had left home, I was no longer working at home, and now the sister that she was closest to was a thousand miles away. For the first time in her life she was home alone after school every day. She was feeling lost and abandoned, and I felt like I needed to keep her close, to protect her. I didn't want to disrupt her life any further by bringing a strange girl into our lives, but I wanted very much to find a way to honor Ms. Rudel's request. There were plenty of options for ways to get involved at South High. It is still known for its diversity of educational opportunities—from its exemplary academic, fine arts, and world languages programs to its resources to help troubled teens finish school.

After some thought, I decided to volunteer to teach a creative writing class in the Mother Infant Care Education program (MICE), the school's program for teen parents. Ms. Rudel and the director of the program agreed, and with the help of my friend Julie Landsman, who had recently published a memoir about teaching in an alternative school, I developed a ten-week course that I was pretty proud of.

When I entered the classroom on the first day, I was surprised and pleased to see that, countering stereotypes, the students were not all Black and were not all girls. There were several responsible, caring young fathers who were in the program with their babies' mothers.

The first two weeks were tougher than I anticipated. Those kids' daily lives were full of chaos. Some were in foster homes with their babies; some still lived at home, and whether or not they felt supported by their parents, they were responsible for the care of their child or children. Some were emancipated and were trying to work, pay rent, and go to school. Some of the girls were in unhealthy relationships and couldn't imagine a different way to live. The teacher told me in advance that she never knew from one day to the next who would show up.

Creative writing was the furthest thing from those students' minds. Nevertheless, I tried to connect with them. I used prompts Julie suggested that had been successful for her. I also used prompts I had designed based on things I heard the students say to each other and to Sue, their teacher. I also came up with prompts based on items I saw in the classroom: colorful posters of famous people or nature scenes with inspirational quotes scrawled across the bottom in large, decorative fonts; pictures of celebrated elders or smiling babies; and items strewn randomly around the room. But nothing worked. I was not able to interest them.

One day one of the girls cleared her throat and gave her glasses a gentle nudge to keep them from sliding down her nose. "Um, Ms. Holbrook," she said. "You're nice, but this is boring! No disrespect, but you don't know nothin' about us. Why you think you can come in here and help us by trying to make us write about things that don't mean nothin' to us?" Around the table, heads nodded in agreement, and I suddenly realized that in my effort to be professional and to avoid disappointing Ms. Rudel, I had denied those young women and men the very thing they needed from any adult who worked with them—to just be my authentic self, to just be real. I made a split-second decision to drop the lesson plan I had so carefully put together and to come clean, show them that I knew more about them than they thought—that the reason I wanted to work with them was because I was one of them. I had my first child when I was seventeen.

I closed the page on the book of poems I had planned to use for the day's prompt and looked from one student to another: the light-skinned black girl who was unable to see her own beauty and her partner, Corey, who adored her and their baby; the blonde girl whose seven-month fetus bore down on her bladder causing her to get up every few minutes to use the restroom, thankfully located in the classroom; and then to the teacher, who nodded slightly, wondering how I would handle the situation.

"I wasn't one of the popular girls in school," I told them and went on to say that I didn't wear pretty dresses or go to school dances, like the Central High Prom or the swanky debutante ball like my sister Joanne. Nor was I surrounded by adoring boys like Joanne and her friends always were. Secretly, I wanted to be like my sister, but it simply wasn't in the cards for me. My personality wasn't the type that attracted popularity. Instead, my friends and I got into fights and talked back to our parents and teachers. And the boys in our south side neighborhood pretty much ignored us.

My mother and stepfather were strict, but one thing my siblings and I were allowed to do without supervision was to take the bus downtown for Saturday afternoon matinees. My friends and I looked forward to those weekly excursions because a group of boys from the north side projects also went to those movies. It was 1961, and they reminded us of the gangs in *West Side Story*; the rough, sexy white boys we saw on reruns of James Dean movies; and of Sidney Poitier, the gorgeous actor from the Bahamas who played Greg in *Blackboard Jungle.* And, unlike the south side boys, they liked us.

Before the 1960s, when I became a teenager, the north side was like a family. Everyone looked out for each other. It didn't matter if you lived in the projects or in one of the middle-class homes near the projects. But by the time we were in our teens, the projects had become more isolated, with poor Black, Native, and Mexican families making up the majority of its residents. We were forbidden to go over north, which made the boys from the projects all the more intriguing. We often lied to our parents, telling them we were going to the movies, and spent Saturday afternoons with the project boys instead. It wasn't long before I fell in love with a boy named Lonnie. He embodied what we saw in the movie bad boys, and I found him utterly intoxicating—the way he shaped his words in a rough, raspy voice that seeped out of the left side of his mouth, his upper lip turned up in a permanent grimace. And the crackling energy he exuded when he moved with a badass swagger was irresistible. He was so full of life and so daring—so different from the sons of the Black bourgeoisie whom my sister attracted and our parents expected us to date and eventually marry.

Even though I wasn't a model teenager, I wanted my

parents' approval. I was sure they would like Lonnie if only they would meet him. Boy, was I wrong! They made it unmistakably clear that they didn't want him coming around, did not want me to see him under any circumstances. But like teenagers since the beginning of time whose parents tried to keep them apart, we found ways to be together. Lonnie had a car and he would pick me up after school several days a week. We made out in his car and made plans for later in the night before he dropped me off a block away from home. "Meet me in the alley," he would say before speeding off, promising to call from the pay phone near my home when he arrived later, after my family was asleep.

Joanne and I had a pink Princess phone that sat on a nightstand between our beds. Luckily, she always fell asleep first. So on the nights Lonnie was going to call, I was able to slip under the covers with my clothes on and hide the phone under my pillow with no worry that she would hear it ring. Like clockwork, his call always came right before midnight. "Ready, baby?" he rasped and then whispering as though he feared that Joanne would hear him, "I'll be there in five minutes."

My bed rested against the wall by our bedroom window, which made my next steps easy. I quietly placed the phone back in its cradle and returned it to the nightstand, glancing over to make sure Joanne was still sleeping. Then I slowly opened the window and crawled out onto the slanted roof and closed the window, leaving it open just a crack to ensure that I would be able to get back in. I'd jump down from the roof and creep out to the alley where Lonnie was waiting.

We never stayed out longer than an hour or two. I wanted to be sure I was back in bed in my pajamas before my family or our neighbors woke up. But one night, Lonnie said he had been watching a small gas station that was open late. The guy who worked there seemed bored and weary, so Lonnie assumed he would be easy prey. He said was going to teach me to drive his old two-tone Buick. I knew he meant that I would drive the getaway car. Something inside of me trembled in fear at that thought—but only for a moment. The biggest part of me was excited, knowing I was about to become a bad guy's girl like Maria and Anita in *West Side Story.*

We drove around an empty lot until Lonnie felt confident that I could handle the Buick. Then he drove to the gas station and parked a few houses away. He got out, leaving the engine idling, then kissed me. "You know what to do." I slid over to the driver's seat, heart pounding, shoulders tense. With sweaty palms gripping the steering wheel, I began to question what I was getting myself into. Sure, it was thrilling, but what if we got caught? Was jail as romantic as the movies made it seem? Was this boy worth the possible consequences?

I didn't have much time to wonder. Soon, a noise that sounded like popcorn popping came from the gas station and Lonnie ran out holding a pistol. He jumped into the passenger seat and I took off. We didn't get very far before we heard sirens blaring and saw red and blue lights flashing in the rearview mirror.

THE YOUNG PARENTS stared in amazement when I told them how that night resulted in my being sentenced to the Minnesota Home School for Girls in Sauk Centre, about a hundred miles northwest of Minneapolis. The doctor there soon discovered that I was three months pregnant and, because of the heart murmur I was born with, sent me back to Minneapolis to spend the remaining six months of my pregnancy incarcerated on the maternity ward at the University of Minnesota Hospital in a bland room with white walls, a cold linoleum floor, and four beds. A steady stream of women came in with labor pains and left within a few days with their newborns. There were also long-term patients, juvies like myself, and women who were there because of difficult medical problems.

I will always remember Dorothy, a woman I became close to who stayed for three or four weeks before her baby was due. She had a weak heart and explained that the doctors wanted to ensure that she would be strong enough when it was time for her to give birth. She went into labor one morning the week before my baby was due. When her husband arrived, I watched him take her hand as she was rolled out of the room. He turned and offered me a smile that contained a mixture of excitement and fear. Sometimes I am still haunted by the helpless look on his face when he returned alone later to pick up her things, his shoulders slumped, his face a flood of tears. Despite reassurances by doctors, nurses, and my social worker that my heart murmur wasn't nearly as serious as Dorothy's condition, I wasn't able to sleep until my son, Stevie, was born on April 23, 1962, and he and I were pronounced healthy.

Tongues clucked and grunts gurgled from the students' throats when I told them that my mother and stepfather wouldn't let me bring my baby home. I had no choice but to put him in foster care or give him up for adoption. I chose foster care. However, I was only allowed to see him once a week, on Saturday afternoons, one hour at a time, for the first fourteen months of his life. Before my mother passed away, I asked her why. "We were afraid of Lonnie,"

she explained, saying that they didn't think they would
be safe if little Stevie and I were in the home and he had
ready access to us.

I was awarded custody of Stevie on my eighteenth
birthday, but I didn't have a clue how to be a parent. Back
then, teen parents didn't have programs like MICE to help
us learn parenting skills. I had already dropped out of
school and, with less than a high school education, struggled to keep a roof over our heads, cleaning with a motel
housekeeping service to supplement my monthly welfare
check and selling high-end cosmetics to wealthy white
women in Minneapolis suburbs. Trying to manage my
frustration was hard. There was so much I didn't understand about babies, and all I knew about being a mother
was the example I was raised with. Keep the child clean
and fed, but when he needed emotional nourishment,
spank him first. It was all the more difficult because Stevie
didn't have a clue who I was, this stranger who until now
he had only seen on those brief weekly visits.

When Stevie was three years old, I packed up our few
belongings and with only eighteen dollars in my pocket
took a Greyhound bus to Springfield, Massachusetts, to
live with my father and his second family for a while. In
many ways, it was a good move. Dad and my stepmother
had two daughters. They were gentle people, and for the
first time in my life I saw children being treated with love
and kindness. I was grateful to see that there was a different way to treat children from the way I had been raised.
This is not meant to be a criticism of my mother and stepfather: I truly believe people raise children the way they
understand. My mother's childhood was difficult. She had
lost both of her parents by the time she was in her early
teens and spent the remainder of her childhood separated

from her siblings, forced to live with unloving relatives. I can only imagine the extent of what she suffered.

THE STUDENTS LISTENED in silence as I told them the next part of my story, the part where I moved to Boston once I was on my feet to find work, and to follow my dream of getting involved in the arts. When Stevie was seven, I married a man I met in an arts program. My child and I experienced unbelievable violence at his hands. If you have read Ntozake Shange's choreopoem *For Colored Girls Who Have Considered Suicide When the Rainbow Is Enuf,* or if you saw Tyler Perry's film adaptation, you no doubt cringed and maybe gasped, cried, or screamed when the Lady in Red's boyfriend, Beau Willie, hung her two children by their ankles from the living room window in their high-rise apartment in the projects, then dropped them, killing them. But as horrifying as it was, you probably thought it couldn't be real, that it was just an overly dramatic scene in a play. I'm here to tell you that such scenes are very real. It's very likely that they occur more often than anyone knows. The man I was married to hung my son from a sixth floor window by his ankles to strengthen a point he wanted to make after having beaten me bloody. And that was just one incident.

Clearly, the brief time of peace I had experienced in my father's home wasn't enough to instill a new sense of positive self-worth in me. It took me ten years to find my way out of that marriage. We moved from Boston to New York City and then to his hometown in North Carolina. The beatings continued, and over time I gave birth to three more of my children, feeling more trapped with each birth.

A surprising turn of events eventually showed me the

way out. One Sunday morning our small church's pianist was sick and couldn't make it to the service. Remembering my childhood piano lessons at Phyllis Wheatley Settlement House in North Minneapolis, I made a feeble attempt to try playing the songs. Afterward, some of the elderly women in the congregation encouraged me to practice, and before long I was able to relieve the pianist from time to time. After a while, I decided to go back to school and earn a GED, which boosted my confidence even more. And finally, scary as it was, I made a decision to strike out on my own, to return to Minneapolis, now a single mother with a new struggle—to raise four kids on my own and a fifth child, Ebony, who would arrive a year later, the result of a failed attempt to reinvigorate a relationship with an old boyfriend.

I DEFINITELY HAD the young parents' attention now. Questions flowed one after the other, most centering on why I had stayed in an abusive relationship for so long, how I dug myself out of poverty, and how I got where I am now, in this classroom with them.

I answered all of their questions candidly and was especially thrilled to tell them about Miss Johnson, my eighth grade English teacher. She played a major role in my eventual return to education. Miss Johnson had somehow made me feel like she saw more in me than just a girl who so often gave teachers good reasons to send her to the principal's office, or to simply ignore me, making me feel invisible. She always had a smile for me when I entered her classroom, and she enjoyed the poems I wrote in her class. And even though there are a lot of well-educated people in my family, she was the first person to make me feel like I might someday be college material myself. Her belief in me stayed in the back of my mind throughout my years of struggle. She is the reason why today I look for the light in the students I work with at the private college and the community college where I have taught. Because of Miss Johnson, I know how important it is to focus on that light, even though it may only be shining dimly when students first enter my classroom. I know firsthand that a spark I light may someday catch fire. I also know that, like Miss Johnson, I may not be the one to witness the flames I may have ignited.

AFTER THAT DAY, the mood in the classroom perked up. The students began responding energetically to my prompts, producing lots of interesting work. And our conversations about our lives continued.

One of the young fathers in the class was a quiet, rather surly young man named Andy, who never wrote or participated in our discussions. He also never missed a class. Andy seemed more sullen than usual the day after then–Speaker of the House Newt Gingrich announced the Republican right wing's so-called Contract with America, which among other things suggested that the nation could reduce the welfare rolls by placing the children of welfare mothers in orphanages. The idea was to prohibit states from paying welfare benefits to children whose paternity was not established and also to the children who were born out of wedlock to women under eighteen years of age. The savings, according to this proposal, would be used to establish and operate orphanages and group homes for unwed mothers.

The morning Andy read about the Gingrich proposal,

he sat planted in his seat, legs crossed, arms folded tightly across his chest, his thick blonde eyebrows furled in a deep frown and his lips glued together in a scowl, all making him look much older than his seventeen years. Then, in the middle of a writing exercise in which, as usual, he had not participated, he suddenly blurted out, "I'm tired of the way people like Newt Gingrich and doctors and social workers treat us. I wanna write a letter to the editor!"

A brief silence came over the classroom, followed by agreement from the other students—all who had experienced offensive treatment by doctors and social workers and even some of their teachers. Sue, the MICE teacher, joined in, confirming that she could tell by a student's demeanor if they had come to class from an appointment or a class that hadn't gone well. And now Newt Gingrich and his "Moral Majority" were insulting them again by promoting a plan that would exacerbate the nearly unbearable restrictions that teen parents were already living under. For instance, for the few hundred dollars they received every month in a check and an electric benefit card to cover only the bare necessities, they had to spend inordinate amounts of time doing paperwork to continue proving month after month that they were qualified—time that ate into the hours they could be caring for their children and completing their homework so they could prepare for self-sufficiency.

Moved by their passion, I once again tossed out my lesson plan. I didn't have a clue how to teach anyone how to write a letter to the editor, but I knew someone who did. The previous summer I had served as interim editor of the *Whittier Globe,* my neighborhood's newspaper, and had put together a series of community journalism workshops taught by seasoned feature writers, sports writers, food critics, and others. One of the journalists was Eric Ringham, then commentary editor at the *Minneapolis Star Tribune.* I called Ringham and was happily surprised by his response. I had hoped he would give me a few pointers, but instead he offered to visit the class the following week, saying that what the kids really needed was instruction on how to write commentary and an effective opinion piece.

When Mr. Ringham came to visit, he went much further. He gave the students a deadline and promised to publish all of the commentaries that were completed by then, and to pay each student whose work he published $100. I would work with them in the weeks after his visit to help them revise their work and prepare the commentaries for publication.

While he explained his work at the *Star Tribune* and his expectations for their commentaries, and even during a writing exercise he gave them, he couldn't help noticing a young woman who kept laying her head on her desk. He called her out on her behavior, letting her know that he thought she must have been bored or just plain rude. She replied that neither was true: she was tired. The journalist in him took over and he became curious, wanted to hear her story.

"Why are you so tired?" he asked.

"I overslept and missed my bus so I walked to school," she replied with a yawn.

No big deal, I'm guessing he thought to himself. But he asked the next question anyway.

"How far do you live from school?"

"Twenty blocks."

Now Ringham was even more curious. "Why didn't you catch the city bus or just stay home?"

"I didn't have any money and I need to get my education."

A dumbfounded look came over his face. He stared at the girl for a moment and then asked when her baby was due.

"Next month," she replied and placed her head back on her desk.

Later, Ringham told me that those kids, especially that young mom who wanted her education so badly that she had walked twenty blocks to school in the eighth month of her pregnancy, changed his view of teen parents. Until then he, like so many others, had bought into the myth that teenagers like them are lazy and promiscuous, uninterested in educating themselves or their children. The intelligence and determination he witnessed that day caught him by surprise.

The students eagerly spent the next few weeks revising their essays. Andy, thrilled that he had been taken seriously, fully participated, taking ownership of the project by sharing valuable feedback on his classmates' work and prodding them through the revision process while he also wrote his own commentary.

The article, "Kids with Kids: Teenage Parents Find Power in the Pen," was published in the *Minneapolis Star Tribune* on Sunday, September 17, 1995, and a few days later we celebrated. Sue brought treats and the kids showed up with their $100 checks in hand, along with a few choice words about negative letters to the editor that had followed the publication. Most of the letters were positive, but I guess it was unrealistic to expect that some readers wouldn't slam the paper for encouraging those awful little slackers by giving them (gasp) money to buy expensive sneakers. Sue and I drew the kids' attention to the letters that praised their determination and those that showed that some readers were inspired and enlightened by their words.

And I learned that by coming clean myself, I had inspired students to find their own voices.

3

TANIA'S BIRTHDAY

*If somebody's buttering you up, you can be
sure they're fixin' to take a bite.*

—Anonymous

It is all too easy for children in a large family to get lost in
the crowd of siblings and grow up believing that they are
not special. It is equally difficult for the parents of large
families to think of their children as individuals rather
than an often overwhelming group. This is especially true
in single-parent homes, because the parent is distracted
trying to keep from losing their mind struggling to make
ends meet, while dealing with each child's needs and personality. All of this is compounded if the relationship with
their co-parent is shaky.

That was how it felt for me after I became a single
mother. So in 1979, about a year after I settled into post-
divorce life, I started looking for ways to spend time alone
with each of my five children so that each of them would
know they were valued. I eventually decided that the best
way was to take one of them on my monthly trip to the
grocery store and to K-Mart, where I shopped for items I
wasn't allowed to purchase with food stamps. I looked forward to the day when I would no longer need food stamps
and the small monthly check I received to supplement the

earnings from my home-based secretarial service. But the check and those food stamps were a welcome help, even with the humiliations I had to endure every month doing paperwork and meeting with social workers who wouldn't look at me and who talked down to me.

I made that decision in December, so our Mommie and Me days would officially begin in January. I wrote *January, February, March, April,* and *May* on pieces of paper, then folded them and placed them in a bowl. I then wrote each child's name on the wall calendar in my home office, one name on the first Saturday of every month according to the month they drew from the bowl. In the months after, it was both amusing and heartwarming to watch the kids take what they thought was a sneak peek at the calendar when the end of a month drew near, to see whose Mommie and Me day was coming up.

Twelve-year-old Tania had drawn the first Mommie and Me day. Like every morning, I got up early on the first Saturday in January to lounge in bed with a cup of coffee and my journal before the kids got up. They know not to disturb me during my quiet time, but anticipation of our time together caused Tania to wake up early. She has a way of slipping into my room as quietly as a panther, crawling under the covers on what she calls the "passenger side" of my bed, then purring so softly as she wanders back to sleep that I hardly know she's there.

I woke her again at 8:00, and by 9:30 we were bundled up and ready to take on the first Saturday morning of Minnesota's most treacherous month. Outside, the day was gray, a sure sign that it wouldn't be as cold as it would be if the sun were shining. We walked to the corner and stepped gingerly over a patch of ice that lined the curb, then found our rhythm by the time the Pearsons' brown-

and-white spotted mongrel wagged his tail and barked his friendly "Good morning." We trekked up Blaisdell Avenue, grateful that the homeowners and landlords had shoveled from yesterday's snowstorm so we could maintain an uninterrupted pace until we reached Butler Drugstore on Twenty-sixth and Nicollet.

Tania and I have always enjoyed silence together as much as conversation. That morning we communed peacefully as we took in the aromas of freshly brewed coffee and bacon and eggs that sneaked through the closed windows of the houses and apartment buildings we passed. We laughed as we listened to the rhythm our boots made with each footfall and watched our breath float away as it seeped through the scarves that covered our mouths.

I always learned something new about my kids on our Mommie and Me days. As the child ambled or skipped along beside me, it was enlightening to find out what they were thinking, how they viewed their particular world. On that January day, Tania was concerned about her grades. We were both disappointed in her performance in school. I couldn't figure out why the most academically gifted of my children was heading for a D in Science and an F in English.

Finally we made it to the drugstore. Just as I pulled my gloved hand out of my coat pocket and was about to reach for the door handle, Tania said, "I'm tired of getting the same old grades all the time."

I looked up at my tall, lovely daughter and wondered where this conversation was going to go. Sometimes I am still amazed when I remember that she had grown taller than me at such a young age. It's clear that she takes after her father's side of the family, who are all over six feet tall.

"Well, dear, I don't think you'll have to worry about that this year." She ignored my sarcastic tone.

"No, Mom, that's not what I mean." Her voice sounded like tinkling bells, even when she was whining. "All they ever give us are A's, B's, C's, D's, or F's. I'd just like to get an H or an M or maybe a P or a Q, for a change."

I could tell by the way she said it that this was a serious matter to her. She is a sensitive girl and would be hurt if I let the laughter I was feeling escape from my lips.

I continued to ruminate on the issue of grades while we sat in the warmth of the drugstore, sipping our hot chocolate. Tania's question made me think about this in a new way, as conversations with my children so often do. It hadn't occurred to me until now to wonder why the people who designed the grading system followed the logical order from A through D, skipped E, and went directly to F. I simply accepted it. Now, like Tania, I wondered why they don't switch the letters up every now and then. It might give kids incentive to try a little harder if they knew they might see an M or a P or a Q on their next report card.

WE SIPPED OUR DRINKS SLOWLY, savoring the warmth of the drugstore, and listened to the post-holiday chatter that was going on around us until we shored ourselves up enough to face the cold again.

Once inside K-Mart, I grabbed a cart and set my purse inside the child seat where I placed my kids when they were toddlers. Christmas songs still blared over the loudspeakers, interrupted occasionally by a scratchy voice that announced the day's Blue Light Special.

We took our time shopping, strolling down every aisle glancing at some items and stopping to inspect others. When we reached the sporting goods section, Tania suddenly stopped.

"Mom, it's still here!"

"What's still here?"

"The ten-speed I showed Dad."

I turned around and there it was, the metallic green bike with *Schwinn* soaring along the crossbar in hot pink—and it was marked down 40 percent. I thought for a moment and calculated the numbers in my head. If I handled my finances well and if we didn't have any emergencies, I could finish paying for the bike by April 27, her thirteenth birthday. I backed it out of its place in the bike rack and Tania happily rolled it to the layaway counter.

OVER THE NEXT FEW MONTHS, she asked several times if she would have the bike in time for her birthday. Each time, I gave her a vague response. What if something happened and I wasn't able to get it out? I didn't want her to be disappointed or to feel like I had lied to her. Besides, I wanted to surprise her.

Happily, I was able to finish paying for the bike in time for her birthday, which I let her celebrate with a Friday night slumber party. I got the kids off to school that morning, then made my way to K-Mart as soon as they opened their doors. I made the final payment and bought enough matching ribbon to make an enormous bow to tie onto the handlebars, then hopped on the bike and rode it home.

Excited for her slumber party, Tania bounced through the door after school with her two best friends, Heather and Ruthie. The oohs and ahhs I heard as she and her two friends stroked the bike made me smile, even though I was irritated with Ruthie, who as always bragged that whatever Tania had, she had something better.

The day was bright and sunny so Tania took the bike for a few spins around the block. I joined Ruthie and Heather on the front porch, cheering each time she flew past the house screaming with her arms flung in the air like she was riding a roller coaster.

Usually, when one of my kids has a sleepover, the others spend the night with one of their friends, always happy to enjoy a night away from home. So by 7:00, most of Tania's guests had arrived and her siblings had left for their own adventures. Just as I finished popping popcorn, I thought I heard a knock on the door. But I wasn't sure. The room my three daughters share is next to the kitchen, which sometimes makes it difficult to hear what's going on in the front of the apartment. Especially when there is a group of teenagers in the room giggling and talking loudly.

I took the popcorn in to the girls, then made my way down the narrow hallway, glancing into our other two bedrooms and the bath with its makeshift shower. I was satisfied that all of the rooms were sparkling clean and hoped that the salty aroma of the popcorn covered the lingering odor of the spray I used to keep the cockroaches down when I had scrubbed and dusted earlier that day.

When I reached the living room, I rested my hand on the doorknob and paused briefly to inspect the sparsely furnished room. Though the kids and I had lived there since my divorce, I was still caught off guard whenever I noticed how the chocolate-brown carpet made the whole apartment seem dark, even on a sunny day or when all the lights are on.

I took a deep breath and opened the door to a smiling thirteen-year-old who introduced herself as Caitlyn.

Blonde and buck-toothed, the girl was a replica of the man who accompanied her. I invited the pair in and directed the girl to Tania's room, then turned back to her father, who stood frozen in the doorway staring at me, his mouth agape. I wondered for a moment if maybe I should call Caitlyn back. Maybe she hadn't told her parents that the girl who was throwing the slumber party was Black. I quickly dismissed that thought. Tania's guests reflected the makeup of our neighborhood, which was very diverse, both racially and economically. The families were used to communicating with people who were different from themselves, and the children played together and visited each other's homes all the time.

Unsure of what to do, I looked down at my feet and waited for the man to speak, feeling certain that the uncomfortable silence was amplified by the stench of mildew that characterized the old fourplex.

Finally he cleared his throat. "I believe I know you," he said with surprise in his voice.

I looked up at the lean, neatly dressed man and searched his face to see if there was anything familiar about him.

"Weren't you in University Hospital about twenty years ago?" he asked.

My oldest son, twenty-five-year-old Steven, was born at the University of Minnesota Hospital, but how did he know this? I continued searching his face but still nothing rang a bell.

"It was twenty-five years ago. My oldest son was born there," I said.

He stood there a moment longer and then said, "Do you remember an intern named Ben? Visited with you almost every day."

I scanned my memory. Nothing came to mind at first but then, as clearly as if it was happening now, I saw myself sitting up in a hospital bed wearing a pink bed jacket my mother had bought me. *There is someone in the chair beside my bed, a chubby white guy with a blonde crew cut and a bad case of acne. "Whoops," he laughs and drops a knight from a chess set onto the blanket that covers my legs. When he leans over to pick it up, I say, "Stop it, Grease!" I slap his hand and then I burst out laughing, too.*

"That was me!" the man almost shouted.

The man at my door looked very different from the guy who used to visit me in the hospital so long ago. This one was tall and slim, his hair was neatly cut and his skin clear.

"How did you recognize me?"

"You haven't changed at all." A wistful look washed over his eyes. "You were the most beautiful creature I had ever seen. I came to visit you nearly every day, even on my days off. Almost got myself in trouble," he said with a chuckle.

I stared at him, flabbergasted. I was beginning to feel very uncomfortable.

Just then my neighbor who lived across the hall came into the building carrying a bag of groceries. She eyed the man suspiciously. I greeted her as she unlocked her apartment door, hoping the hint of desperation in my voice would make him go away.

"I remember dropping things on your bed just so I could touch you," he said. "Marveled at your dark skin, so different from mine." Then he shook his head and walked away, leaving me dumbfounded. I floated back to the kitchen to unwrap the frozen pizzas I had planned to make for the girls, stopping at the bathroom for a quick glance in the mirror.

Me . . . beautiful?

When I was a child I didn't see myself as beautiful or smart. My siblings and I took piano lessons and dance classes, but our parents did not encourage our creativity or our individuality. That puzzled me because my stepfather, Barney, played guitar professionally. Mom was also creative. She made our clothes and was imaginative in the kitchen. But whenever they saw me reading a book for pleasure or writing a poem, or just sitting and thinking, they would chide me.

"You better stop all that daydreaming. You're gonna have to work twice as hard and be twice as smart as white girls if you want to get anywhere in this world."

In addition to their creativity, my parents were both successful professionals in their day jobs. Mama owned a beauty salon and Barney was the first Black auditor for the Minnesota Department of Agriculture. Now that I am an adult with children of my own, I understand their concern. I know their concerns were based on history and their own experiences. They had to pay a heavy price for their successes.

It is hard to immunize ourselves against the racism America was built on. Looking back, I can see how the self-hatred of internalized racism played out in many ways in our home. It wasn't unusual to hear Barney say something about someone who "can't talk" during dinnertime conversations, referring to someone they had seen at a party or a Black person on television whose speech patterns or dialect showed that they were not well educated. Nor was it unusual for Mama to say something about families who lived in the projects.

Conversations that focused on skin color were not rare. I remember an incident at Mama's beauty shop when

I was about twelve years old. Beauty and barber shops have always been places where folks in the Black community gather to relax and let their hair down, literally and figuratively. Typical of 1950s beauty salons, Mama's shop smelled like chemicals and old grease and sparkled with the sounds of laughter, hand-clapping, and clicking curling irons. That day I flopped into the chair, dreading the familiar operation that I knew was coming when Mama, dressed in the crisp white uniform that hairdressers wore back then, wrapped a plastic cape around my shoulders and tied it behind my neck. Then she picked up a straightening comb and placed it in the stove that heated her straightening combs and curling irons.

Mrs. King, a large woman who was always there to spread the latest gossip, said, "Yeah, girl, she sure shoulda known better, black as that niggah is."

Mama pried the bright red top off of a black-and-white can with *Madame Belva's Hair-Rep* printed across the front in large letters, its name promising to fix hair that was somehow bad and in need of repair. In went two fingers, then out they came, carrying a blob of thick grease. She smoothed it into my hair section by section, to make it easier for the hot comb to slide through the sizzling grease from the roots to the ends of my hair, making it straight as a stick. Just as she turned the chair around so I was facing the mirror, Mrs. King said, "Got them red eyes, too. You know he got to be evil. But she black too, so I guess they understand each other."

Laughter exploded all around me. Everyone in the shop—the other hairdressers, their clients, and the other women who, like Mrs. King, were there just to pass the time away—howled as though it was the funniest thing they had ever heard. I looked at the reflections of myself and my mother standing behind me, and Mrs. King, whose wide hips drooped over the seat of her chair. Mama's skin, and Mrs. King's, reminded me of peaches, but my skin is cinnamon brown. Compared to them and my sister Joanne, I felt black as coal.

That glance in the mirror convinced me that I was fighting a losing battle just by being alive. It wouldn't matter how smart I was or hard I tried; I would never be respected, neither by whites nor by my own people.

BY THE TIME I reached my mid-teens I was mad at the world, determined to do the opposite of anything my parents wanted me to do. My girlfriends and I started hanging out in the projects, and I had fallen in love with Lonnie, which led to the October night that landed me in the University of Minnesota Hospital's maternity ward.

On arrival at the hospital I was placed in an empty room with four beds, one that would be my home for the next six months. I changed into a hospital gown and crawled under the covers quaking with fear. I listened to footsteps up and down the hallway outside my door; the efficient sound of nurse's squishy rubber soles, the clicking high heels of female visitors, sometimes alongside male companions whose steps sounded sturdier. What was going to happen to me here, I wondered? This hospital was not new to me. I was born with a heart murmur, and my mother had been taking me to the heart clinic since I was a little girl. But I had never seen any of their patient rooms, and this was the first time I had seen a maternity ward anywhere.

Because the University Hospital is a teaching hospital, many women shared my room during my stay, all for short periods of time—a few hours, a few days, some for a few weeks. Some were rich, some were poor; most were from cities, towns, and rural areas around Minnesota, a few were from other countries. Most were there because, like me, they had medical conditions that needed to be watched. I was the only one who was there because of a judge's sentence, and I was the only one with dark skin.

Throughout my six-month incarceration, I attended daily occupational therapy sessions, and a teacher came once a week to keep me current with my eleventh grade studies. I was grateful for those activities as they allowed me a little bit of time away from my makeshift jail cell. I was also happy when my older sister Joanne came to see me. Ever since we were children, she always made me feel safe and cared for. But I dreaded Mama and Barney's visits. They often brought me gifts, but Mama's hurtful, accusing words and Barney's disapproving scowls negated the love that those gifts should have represented.

During one of their visits, Mama and Barney told me I couldn't bring my baby home. "Why?" I asked through bitter tears. Instead of answering they said something like, "We think you know why." But I didn't know why.

Their refusal to let me bring the baby home set off a rush of visits from social workers who came with the purpose of persuading me to give my baby up for adoption. My primary social worker, Mrs. McGarrett, was a cross-eyed, thick-boned woman with yellow teeth. I laugh now when I think back on the dowdy woolen coat she always wore and the crown-shaped hat that sat at an angle over the salt-and-pepper bun pinned furiously at the back of her neck, making it look like her hat might topple off her head at any moment.

I never knew when Mrs. McGarrett was going to show

up. The only warning was the unmistakable sound of her heels marching down the hall to my room. She would plop down in the chair beside my bed and look around, taking note of whoever was sharing my room. Then she would turn her attention to me and launch into her spiel, gesticulating stiffly with her right arm. "Off with her head," her gesture seemed to command minions that only she could see, causing me to cross my arms tightly over my chest, refusing to look at her. Instead, I would lean back against the two thin pillows that propped me up in bed and dare her invisible gang of knaves to try it. No one was going to take my baby away from me, no one was going to convince me to give the baby away, and I'd be damned if anyone was going to chop my head off.

The chubby young intern named Ben with the blond crew cut started visiting around that time. At first he came once a week, then twice, gradually increasing his visits until he was there nearly every day. He read to me and told me silly jokes, taught me to play chess, and listened to my worries. I was happy for his company, thought it was part of his job to spend time with long-term patients.

One day an attractive woman with long brown hair and violet eyes was brought in to wait out the first stages of her labor. The nurses settled her into the bed that faced mine, and as soon as she was comfortable her husband, a doctor I recognized because of his height and booming voice, came in and pulled up a chair beside her. I watched as he kissed her tenderly and stroked her hair, then handed her a textured green, purple, and gray bag he had carried into the room. She reached into the bag and pulled out a pink-and-blue blanket attached to two long skinny needle-like things and a ball of yarn.

I watched in awe as the woman looped a strand of

yarn around the finger of one hand, slid the needle into a loop on the needle she held in her other hand, then looped the yarn around the first needle, and pulled it through. The two long needles clicked rhythmically as she knitted row after row. My mother spent many hours at her sewing machine making clothes for my siblings and me, but this was the first time I had seen anyone knit.

The woman knitted for hours, her face reddening with each contraction until they became too intense. Then she quietly handed the knitting to her husband, who tucked it back into the bag and boomed for an orderly to bring a gurney. They wheeled her out of the room, leaving her knitting bag behind. I waited until I was sure no one was watching, then snuck over to her bed and took the blanket out and studied it for a while, making sure to return it to the bag before the doctor and his wife returned to the room following the birth of their baby.

The next day I asked my occupational therapist to teach me to knit. We laughed through my first attempts. She was right-handed and found it an interesting challenge to help me, a left-hander, pick up the stitches I dropped and place them in the correct spot. It wasn't very long before those first attempts became a long skinny scarf. The first few inches carried the telltale jagged edges characteristic of a new knitter, then gradually changed to edges that were even. Once I got the hang of it, knitting became easy, and I fell in love with it as an art form.

Mrs. McGarrett had the authority to persuade the court to refuse my request for custody of my baby, and she never missed an opportunity to remind me. At first, I hid my knitting from her and my parents, refusing to let them in on something beautiful that I was doing. But I always let them see how well I was doing with my schoolwork, hoping somehow that if they saw that I was a diligent student, they would eventually believe that I could be a responsible mother. But one day about a month before my son was born, I was knitting a pair of booties when Mrs. McGarrett showed up. I decided not to hide them when I heard her marching down the hall.

She sat in the chair beside my bed and watched the yellow yarn slowly take shape. Finally she asked what I was knitting.

"Some booties for my baby," I replied, refusing to look at her.

"Where did you get the yarn?" she croaked, as though it was her business to know.

"Occupational therapy."

She didn't say much more that day, just watched as though she was seeing me for the first time. When she returned the next week, she said she might be able to find a foster home for the baby.

I dropped my knitting needles and turned to face her, noticing a softness in her gray eyes that hadn't been there before. Still, I was suspicious. There had to be a catch.

"We can place the baby in a foster home," she said, "with the understanding that you can have custody once you turn eighteen and are released from the court system. That is, if you stay out of trouble and if you haven't changed your mind by then."

I didn't see the chubby intern again. And I didn't give him another thought until that Friday night when he brought his daughter over for Tania's slumber party.

LATER ON the night of Tania's birthday party, while I was waiting for the pizzas to finish baking, feeling like the unforgettable woman I'd read about in corny love stories, the phone rang. I floated over and picked up the yellow wall phone, humming, "Unforgettable, that's what you are . . ."

I answered with a lilt in my voice. There was a pause on the other end.

"Hello?" I repeated.

The male voice sounded hesitant. "Uh, this is Ben, Caitlyn's dad." He paused again. "I need to ask a favor of you."

"No problem," I replied with a smile in my voice.

"A lot has changed since I was an intern," he said. He had my full attention now, and I had a feeling that my dream was about to end.

"Yeah. A lot has changed in my life, too."

We both laughed nervously.

"I have a family now and I've built a successful practice."

"That's great, Ben," I replied, looking around at the depressing changes that had taken place in my life.

"I need to ask you not to repeat what I said to you earlier."

"What do you mean?"

"Well, if anyone ever found out, my life would be ruined."

I couldn't believe what I was hearing.

"You don't understand." He paused briefly, cleared his throat again, struggled to say something, then hung up.

Incredulous, I stood a moment longer before slamming the phone down. What was really going on with this guy, I wondered?

As I stood there I began to think about something I had seen on episodes of *St. Elsewhere* and *Marcus*

Welby, M.D.—the part where I heard them say something about an oath they had to take, which in part said, "First, do no harm."

When Ben stood in my doorway, he had said, "Almost got myself in trouble." Was that an admission that by spending so much time with a young, pregnant, vulnerable girl whom he had a crush on, he had violated that oath? When he referred to me as a "creature" while defining me as beautiful, had he really seen that young Black girl as a human or was he viewing her as something less than human, perhaps as a toy? Or worse, as a thing that he could violate without giving it a second thought, like the slave owners who violated my foremothers?

So many questions raced through my mind in that moment that I almost forgot about the kids until Tania came into the kitchen with Caitlyn following closely behind her. "Mom, I smell something burning."

Frantically, I grabbed two pot holders and opened the oven door to retrieve the ruined mess. Tania and her friends provided a sad-faced audience as they watched thick, black smoke pour out of the oven while I smoldered inside, like the pizzas. I wanted to cry, but no way was I going to let Caitlyn see that her father had humiliated me. She had no clue what had just happened anyway.

Deflated, I sat down at the kitchen table trying to figure out what to do. I had spent all of my money on the party and didn't expect any more until the first of the month.

Tania was the first to speak. "Do we have any more pizzas?"

"No," I replied, shaking my head.

"I have the money Dad sent me," she said.

"And I have five dollars from babysitting," boasted Ruthie.

All of the girls scrambled through their bags, pockets, and backpacks looking for money they had brought with them.

"I have an idea," announced Heather. "Let's go to McDonald's!"

The girls were freshly excited now with a new, unexpected adventure in the making, and I was relieved. In the midst of the happy screams, Tania asked, "Can I ride my new bike to McDonald's?"

"Yes," I replied, hugging her on our way out the door.

AS I WALKED BEHIND THE GIRLS listening to their chatter, I wondered what their lives might be like when they reached my age. Would things improve for women by then? Would my daughters be confronted with situations like what I had experienced that night? Would Caitlyn? My hope was that they would find the courage within themselves that we women have always had: the courage to know and believe that we exist, we are here, we are powerful, we are strong; the strength to stand up to a world that would continue to try to keep them in the kitchen. But I was still reeling from what had happened. It was nearly impossible to think clearly about how to give those girls anything that might show them strength. It was simply too complicated to deal with in that moment. I made a vow to find a way to do all I could to teach my daughters to stand in their own power.

In the weeks and months that followed, as I continued to ruminate on that night and to try to figure out what I had learned about myself as a result, it became clearer and clearer that even though I still didn't have answers, I knew that our Mommie and Me days showed my children that I valued them. And I hoped that I was teaching my sons to cherish the women who come into their lives as much as they honored their mother and loved their sisters.

And by the way, I wasn't surprised that Caitlyn's mother—not her father—picked her up the morning after Tania's slumber party.

4

THE "AWARD"

*Nothing is more difficult than competing
with a myth.*

—Françoise Giroud

Lawrence Hutera became my boss in 1981, when he helped me start the Whittier Writers' Workshop at Whittier Park and Community Center. He is very proud that in such a short time, W³, as he calls it, has become the talk of the town. So proud, in fact, that he nominated me for a YWCA Leader Lunch Award a couple of months ago. I remember when he told me, it was the first Wednesday in January, the first night of our winter playwriting class.

We had planned to hold the class in the small room where the poetry and journal writing classes had been on Monday and Tuesday. But so many people showed up for the playwriting class that Big Jimmie Smith, whose job is to maintain order in the park, made a last-minute decision to move the class to a larger room.

"We gonna hafta tell 'em to wait a few minutes," Jimmie said in his slow Mississippi drawl, his words spilling over the unlit cigarette that seems to be a part of him, drooping from his mahogany lips. He adjusted the visor of his floppy, blue denim cap and went into the multipurpose room where a group of boys were playing floor hockey.

I directed the registrants to the lounge where they could wait in comfortable chairs around the fire Jimmie had built in the fireplace, instead of having to stand in the lobby and stare at the brick walls that were the color of milk that's about to go sour.

It wasn't long before the kids filed out of the room like stair steps: the smallest first, followed by the middle-sized, and ending with the eldest, Melvin Melby and Melvin Campbell, and a stream of curses. Jimmie Smith is a kindhearted, even tempered brother, but his massive size causes most of the kids who hang out at the park to think twice before messing with him. Not so for "the Melvins," as the eldest of the Melby and Campbell clans are called by park staff.

The Campbells are three freckle-faced caramel-toned Black kids and the Melbys are five red-headed white kids, also with freckles. The Melvins are both twelve years old and the best of friends. They show up every day after school with their little brothers and sisters and cause mayhem until Jimmie throws them out. Their families are saddled with drug and alcohol addiction problems, so we don't want to eighty-six the kids; they don't have another safe place to go after school and may not get anything to eat except for the snacks we serve. Jimmie lets them stay on one condition—that they do their homework before they start playing. He puts them in a quiet room and watches over them until they've all completed their assignments. Many times, I have walked past that room and observed the older boys working with their younger siblings with a tenderness they never show when they think others might be watching. It's also touching to see Jimmie struggling to help them. His education is limited, and he is determined to do all he can to make sure that those children get theirs.

Jimmie didn't leave the kids without options. "Y'all got three choices," he drawled and glanced at his watch. "You can sit in the lounge and play some games, or you can go put on some ice skates and join the skating class that's about to start, or y'all can go home."

"We don't need you," yelled Melvin Campbell as he and Melvin Melby led their siblings out of the building in their threadbare winter coats.

"Don't forget your homework," Jimmie called after them. He then went back into the room, followed by the playwriting instructor and Egon, a regular who takes every class we offer. Some of the other participants were eager to help set up the room as well. I wanted to stop them, wishing the smell of sweaty children would magically disappear before the class began. I was about to suggest that everyone just sit tight when I heard a woman say to her friend, "This is what community's really about, isn't it?" I held my tongue and cringed as I watched them dodge a little boy in a red T-shirt who darted past them as they made their way into the room.

When the class was finally under way, I stepped behind the counter to straighten up the flyers and brochures that announce park programs and other neighborhood events, proud that another of our classes had filled.

JUST AS I FINISHED straightening up the counter and was about to join the playwriting class, Lawrence came out of his office, surprising me. His door had been closed and I didn't know he was there. He sashayed up to me and told me he was going to nominate me for an award.

"You're a natural," he said and handed me the application. *The YWCA Leader Lunch is an annual luncheon that recognizes women whose leadership and contributions have aided in the growth and development of their communities,* it stated in the first paragraph. I read on, taking in the names of past winners: doctors, lawyers, architects, intellectuals, businesswomen, artists, and rich women who spend their time volunteering for nonprofit organizations.

"You must be out of your mind to think I could compete with women like them!" Lawrence is a genius at finding and seizing opportunities, but this time I was sure he had missed the boat.

Lawrence threw his head back, shaking his thick mane—his hair was the color of a ripe apricot that week—and flashed his sparkling smile. He has the straightest teeth I've ever seen. When he laughs they sparkle like a row of diamonds, and crinkles form around his soft gray eyes. His laugh begins deep in his belly, moves up to his throat, and then rushes out of his mouth, resonating throughout the park building.

"Yeah, tell me something new, girlfriend," he laughed. "Everybody knows I'm crazy. But you're a great candidate. I know you'll win." Big Jimmie Smith, who had been talking with me while I straightened up the counter, chuckled and nodded in agreement.

I tried to put it out of my mind, but it wasn't easy. I was sure I wouldn't win the award. But when you know something's out there with your name on it, it's pretty hard not to think about it.

I HAD STARTED W^3 so I could take writing classes I couldn't afford at other places, and I took every class we offered. My dream has always been to be a writer, and when I found myself divorced and the single mother of four children, I decided it was time to pursue my dream. But I got distracted when I ran into an old boyfriend. We tried to pick up where we had left off when we broke up after high school. It didn't work out, but I became pregnant. I considered having an abortion, but my personal moral code wouldn't allow me to go through with it. I am a strong believer in a woman's right to choose. For me, the choice was to have the baby and raise her. So there I was, a thirty-four-year-old single mother with four kids between the ages of eight and sixteen, and a fifth child on the way—a single mom whose only income was a monthly welfare check and food stamps.

The kids and I had moved into the Whittier neighborhood of Minneapolis in 1978, shortly after I realized I was pregnant. I was so depressed I could hardly get out of bed, but I knew my kids needed to meet other children and have a place to play. The park was only a block away from our apartment, easy for the kids to walk to if I wasn't able to go with them. I was really drawn to the place because of Lawrence and Big Jimmie. They greeted my kids and me like we were old friends, instantly making us feel welcome.

Late that summer, I made a decision to find a way to keep from going completely insane. Deciding to make use of the secretarial skills I had learned before dropping out of high school, I rented a typewriter and put an ad for secretarial services in the *Minnesota Daily,* the newspaper of the University of Minnesota. It wasn't long before my phone started ringing off the hook. I taught Julian, Iris, and Tania, who were still in elementary school, how to answer the phone properly and how to help me proofread.

I didn't earn enough to get me off public assistance, but my secretarial service, which I called Carolyn &

Associates, was successful enough to supplement the monthly checks and food stamps. My conversations with my social worker took on a different tone, supportive and respectful. Soon I was able to purchase my own typewriter and I taught the children to type. Back in 1978, the IBM Correcting Selectric was a popular typewriter. Mine was custom ordered, hot pink. Whenever I was questioned, my reply was simple and straightforward: "If I'm going to pay their price, I mize well get what I want."

My depression recurred after Ebony was born that November. It became so severe that I was hospitalized. But the intended month-long hospitalization was reduced to a week when one of sixteen-year-old Stevie's friends came to our home with a full-blown case of chicken pox. The woman whom the welfare department sent to care for my children left, fearing that she would contract the disease. I had no choice but to come home. I made a conscious decision to try not to focus on my situation—living alone with five children in an awful apartment infested with mice and cockroaches. I decided instead to try taking it a day at a time with hopes that I could someday find my way out. I also started taking long walks and journaling. I began writing for my neighborhood newspaper, the *Whittier Globe,* articles that focused on the funny things my children said and did. The articles became a weekly column that I titled "Diary of a Single Mother by Beatrice Mullins." Over the next two years, the column won first- and second-place awards from the Neighborhood Press Association.

Lawrence and his then-partner Bill were among the kindhearted people who helped me get back on my feet. They came over and brought food and helped me see the humor in my situation. They gave me work so my secretarial service wouldn't fail and so I could continue to earn a little money. Eventually, Lawrence let on that the main reason he started getting more involved in our lives was that he saw me as an intelligent, talented woman, and he loved my smart, well-behaved children. He sincerely wanted to help pull me out of my depression.

Eventually, I did brighten up and decided to go back to school. I had earned a GED while living in North Carolina with my ex-husband. Maybe I was ready for college now. I enrolled in Minneapolis Community College. I had permission to hire a day care provider, but the woman I hired proved to be unreliable. I never knew if she was going to show up. I missed too many classes and had to withdraw before my first semester ended. I then looked around for writing classes but wasn't able to find any that I could afford. The welfare department deducted a sizeable portion of my earnings from my monthly check and would only pay for classes if I was pursuing a degree.

Lawrence knew of my desire to write, so he wasn't surprised when I asked if he would consider adding creative writing to the center's adult activities. At first he turned me down. Lawrence is a performing artist and enjoys putting on large, noisy events. He wasn't sure if quiet activities like writing classes would work. But after some thought, he changed his mind. He then put the onus on me to create my own opportunity. "If you can find someone to teach a class," he said, "I will support you."

One day my son Julian came home from school and told me that a poet was visiting his fifth grade class that week. He overheard her telling his teacher that she needed someone to type her manuscript and my sweet son referred her to me. A week later, when the poet brought me her manuscript, I asked if she would be willing to teach a class in our neighborhood community center. She agreed and, true to his promise, Lawrence taught me how to write a press release to advertise the six-week class.

At the time, neither of us knew that the Twin Cities are home to a vibrant literary community. Nor did we know that the teacher, Natalie Goldberg, would later become famous for her books on writing and the workshops she teaches around the country. We thought we would attract a few people from the neighborhood and were surprised that the press release, which Lawrence sent to his extensive media list, attracted people from all over the Twin Cities area. Natalie taught another six-week class and then introduced me to other teaching writers, and before I knew it, I was leading a creative writing program and taking free of charge the classes that we offered to the public—affordable classes taught by professional writers and teachers.

As is often the case when someone gives us a life-changing gift, Natalie doesn't remember me or those workshops. Looking back, the same has been true for me many times since those days. One example that stands out is a day when I was sitting outdoors at a coffee shop with a friend. A young woman approached me and said that she had just completed her master's degree. "It's because of something you said," she told me and reminded me of a writing workshop I had taught for teens in a nonprofit organization where she had been working some years before. She said that while we were waiting for the kids to show up one afternoon, she complained that the men who ran the organization expected her to do all of the grunt work. According to her I said, "Don't let them keep you in the kitchen." Like Natalie Goldberg, I do not remember the young woman or the conversation that led to her return to school. But I'm happy that something I said had such a powerful effect on her.

SOON WE WERE OFFERING CLASSES two nights a week, then three, then four. We held readings at the end of each quarter of classes and occasional poetry/theater performances that combined lines of student poems with scenes from playwriting students' plays-in-progress. We also published *Writer's Cramp,* a booklet of student writings.

Since its inception, W³ attracted people from all over Minneapolis and St. Paul, but few were people of color. I will always be grateful to Cynthia Gehrig, then president of the Jerome Foundation. Because of her enthusiasm and funding from the foundation, we were able to establish a mentoring program for African American writers in the fall of 1984, the first of its kind in the Twin Cities area. With a well-known local author as our mentor, a group of eight emerging writers (including myself) planned to learn together for a season. As it turned out, what I wanted or expected was different from our mentor's expectations, causing the project to turn out differently from what either of us anticipated. The Jerome Foundation helped me understand that some efforts work out better than others. The people at the Jerome Foundation also taught me that clear communication is often the key to a project's success, and they continued to support my efforts both at W³ and in my later endeavors.

Lawrence also continued to mentor me. When he saw how the Whittier Writers' Workshop was growing, he started sending me to classes and workshops on arts administration. We turned W³ into a nonprofit with its own board of directors and the capacity to raise funds independent of the Park Board. I am very proud of what we accomplished. I never dreamed that my efforts to create something that was primarily for me would affect so many people. In just three years from its start, the little writing group I started in an urban park had served nearly a thousand people. And between my children, W³, and my secretarial service, I had plenty to keep me busy, for which I was grateful.

THE CALL CAME ONE MORNING in March around 10:00, while I was sitting at my desk in my home office, typing away at a client's dissertation. I had decided not to answer the phone until I had finished the section I was working on. Besides, I was a little afraid that it might be the client, and I would have to tell him that I wasn't as far along as I had hoped to be by then. Caller ID wasn't readily available at the time, so whenever the phone rang, there was always the niggling fear that something may be wrong with one of the kids at school.

I waited until the phone stopped ringing and the light flashed to indicate that the caller had left a message. I listened to the message and couldn't believe my ears when the friendly voice congratulated me on winning a 1985 YWCA Leader Lunch Award. She said I'd be receiving a formal letter of congratulations in the mail along with an invitation to the luncheon and some instructions.

"See there? What'd I tell you?" smiled Lawrence.

It turned out that the awards committee was so impressed with my work that they wanted to give me an award. They couldn't find a place for my award within their stock categories, so they created a new category,

Neighborhood Impact. I had mixed feelings about that. I'm happy that they thought enough of me to give me this honor, and I'm pleased that my work caused them to think of an important new awards category. Women who are in the trenches, making their neighborhoods better and safer, *should* be honored. But that's not what I felt I was doing with the writers' workshop. I couldn't understand why my award shouldn't have been in the Arts category. It disturbed me that too often Black people are only celebrated if our work is related to the social services. While it is true that W^3 was located in the heart of an urban community, it is also true that its success added another level of status to the Whittier neighborhood. But everything's located somewhere, isn't it? W^3 appeals to people from all over the Twin Cities and has attracted a lot of attention. Not because we are a social service agency, but because our affordable activities increased access to the literary arts for Twin Cities residents.

The awards ceremony was on May 10, 1985. I couldn't sleep the night before. I lay in bed staring at the clock at 4 a.m., my mind racing. How would I handle standing in front of a room full of strangers, giving an acceptance speech? How in the world did I win this award anyway? The only other time I won anything was a stuffed elephant at Dayton's department store. Didn't the awards committee know better? I was sure that if I showed up at the luncheon everyone there—the committee members and the audience—would recognize their mistake. I might even be arrested for daring to show up.

Mornings in our house have always been chaotic, but nothing went well that morning. As usual, thirteen-year-old Iris got up at 4:30 and went into the bathroom, slammed the door, and turned on her boom box. Too tired to yell at her to turn it down, I just lay there and waited for her to bang on my door for our 5:00 session with our favorite television aerobics instructor.

Afterward, I poured a steaming cup of coffee and settled into my journal until ten-year-old Tania banged on the bathroom door, where Iris always hides out for at least another half-hour after aerobics, listening to her heavy metal station.

"Get out of there. I gotta go to the bathroom," screamed Tania.

"Not 'til I'm good and ready," Iris retorted, setting Tania into a burst of angry tears and more banging on the door.

Fourteen-year-old Julian stepped out of his room, across from the bathroom. "What's going on?" he asked, startled. I had planned to let him sleep in this morning since he was going to the luncheon with me. I wanted all of my kids to share my triumph, but the rule was that the honorees could invite only two guests. Anyone else we wanted to bring would have to purchase a $25 ticket. I understand that events are costly. But the way I see it, if you're going to give a woman on public assistance an award, you should make it possible for her to bring her children. It would be very encouraging to them as they think about their own futures. I decided to invite my mother and step-dad and asked them to buy a ticket so I could bring Julian. It was important for him to see the result of his having introduced me to Natalie Goldberg four years ago, when he was in fifth grade.

Things quieted for a moment and then the boom box wars began. Iris went into the kitchen and turned her hard rock back on, competing with Tania's soft rock that was now coming from the bathroom, and Julian's gospel music was going full blast in his room. I gave up and put my journal down and turned off my jazz, which had been playing in the living room. I was sitting on the couch feeling help-less, tired, excited, scared, and a little bit pissed when the phone rang.

"Hi, Mom." It was twenty-two-year-old Stevie.

"Where have you been? I've been worried sick about you!" I hadn't heard from him or seen him in almost a week.

"I'm in Chicago. Can you send me some money so I can get back home?"

"What are you doing in Chicago?"

"Well," he hesitated briefly and then said, "me and my homies were on our way to St. Paul for a party and decided to keep going. Now we don't have any money left."

"And you expect me to send money that I don't have?"

"Aw, Ma, c'mon."

"Look. You found your way down there. I'm sure you can find your way back."

There was a momentary pause on the other end of the line, and I could hear Iris and Tania gearing up for another round.

"You're some kinda mom," Stevie's deep voice was seething with anger.

"Hey," I replied, "I may not be what you asked for, but I'm what you got." He slammed the phone down, and I hung up and rushed into the girls' room to referee, still hearing his deep, accusing voice in my head and knowing that my worry about where he was would now be replaced with worry about whether he would get home safely. But at least his hip hop music wouldn't be added to this morn-ing's boom box chorus.

There was peace after I finally got Iris and Tania off to school. Julian turned off his music and went back to bed. As I was about to pour myself another cup of coffee I dropped and broke my favorite cup—further proof, I was sure, that the day wasn't going to go well.

While I was sweeping up the mess, six-year-old Ebony, who can sleep through nearly anything, came out of her room. Wiping the sleep out of her eyes, she asked what made that noise she just heard. Then she looked around and when she didn't see anyone asked, "Didn't Tania, Iris, and Julian come home last night?"

I had planned to make final revisions to my acceptance speech after getting Ebony off to school but discovered that the cartridge for my pink Selectric had run out and I hadn't bought one to replace it. I wasn't about to deliver a handwritten speech. I certainly didn't want the other winners to think I was tacky in addition to being a welfare mother. Fortunately, we lived on a good bus line, so I was able to make it downtown to the office supply store and get back home quickly enough to finish typing my speech, take a shower, and be ready when Mom and Barney were scheduled to pick Julian and me up. But there wasn't any hot water. I had to take a cold shower.

By the time we got to the Hyatt Regency ballroom I was a wreck. Mom, Barney, and Julian were ushered to a table and I was told to join the other honorees at the head table. I looked at Mom desperately, and she smiled, hugged me, and said, "Remember that old saying—when you look out at the audience, just imagine everyone sitting on the toilet."

I made my way to the platform where the head table sat and stumbled up the two steps, tripping on the top one. A smiling woman greeted me and showed me to my seat. Unsure of what to do with my hands, I looked around to see what the other women were doing, then put my purse and the manila folder that held my acceptance speech under my seat. I wanted to take a sip from the water goblet in front of me in order to try to calm myself, but I was sure I would drop it. I wanted to start in on the salad that smiled up at me but was sure I'd drop pieces of lettuce onto my lap. The women on either side of me tried to make conversation, but all I could do was smile and answer yes or no as I looked at their expensive business suits and compared them to the beige dress I had found on a sale rack at Dayton's. I looked out at the room that was quickly filling up and found my son and my parents and saw Lawrence laughing with someone. I felt comforted and took a few bites of my lunch.

Soon I heard the woman who would emcee the program tell someone that they had counted a thousand people in the audience. She then alerted us that she was about to begin the program. My pounding heart sank to the bottom of my feet and my hands began to sweat. That many people are going to watch me make a fool of myself? Suddenly, I just wanted to get the whole thing over with and go home and crawl into my bed, my hiding place.

I watched the emcee walk confidently to the microphone and heard her graciously thank everyone for being there. I looked out at the audience, and everything began to move in slow motion. One by one, the honorees got up, accepted their awards, and gave their thank-yous. Then it was my turn. I panicked when I realized I had forgotten my speech under my chair. *My son's out there,* I reminded myself. *I can't embarrass him.* I had no choice but to wing it. I stumbled over the first few words, then began to pick up steam once I realized I remembered a lot of what I had intended to say. I was surprised by the power in my voice when I got to the part about how I put on a crash helmet and pushed through the obstacles in my life. I was even more surprised when the audience began to cheer, and I was speechless as I watched person after person, beginning with Lawrence, rise from their seat smiling and clapping.

I ASKED MOM AND BARNEY to let me stop at the supermarket on the way home. I wanted to have something special for dinner so the kids could celebrate with me in some small way. I picked up a couple of steaks and a box of marble cake mix. The cashier's line moved more slowly than I would have expected for a weekday afternoon near the middle of the month. When I made it to the front of the line, I absently put my items on the conveyor. The cashier, a skinny woman with dirty blonde hair, greeted me with a scowl. I waited patiently for her to finish ringing me up, then counted out my food stamps and handed them to her.

"I'm surprised people with food stamps can buy steak," she spat and snatched them out of my hand. I was so shocked that I couldn't speak. She, of course, had no idea why I was using food stamps. For all she knew, I could have been shopping for someone whose medical condition required a high-protein diet. And she obviously had no idea that most mothers who receive welfare checks and food stamps are not the mythical "welfare queens" that Ronald Reagan painted low-income single mothers to be. Rather than collecting massive welfare payments through fraud, child endangerment, or manipulation, most of us, like myself, out of necessity are in this system that shames and humiliates us.

I was taken aback but wanted to hold on to my good mood and whatever dignity remained after the cashier's verbal assault. I stood there for a moment and Julian stepped a little closer and glared at the woman. I took my son's hand, then picked up my bag, straightened my posture, and walked out of the store, head held high, and wondered if winning the award would help to get me off welfare.

5

FINALLY INDEPENDENT

Pray, trust, and do the dishes.

—Kathy Saulton

The YWCA Leader Lunch award didn't get me off welfare, but it certainly made me more determined to figure out how to become self-sufficient. I stayed with W^3 another three years and also continued to grow my secretarial service. But I eventually grew tired of working at home. Tania was about to graduate from high school, Ebony was in middle school, and Iris, Julian, and Stevie had left home to begin their adult lives. I was ready to move on to an outside work environment.

I took a job in one of our neighborhood's social service agencies. I don't remember what position I was hired for, but I remember that I wasn't happy there after working in the arts. I spent a lot of time in the year I worked there questioning the logic of my feelings. Shouldn't I be grateful for this job, to finally be able to tell the welfare department goodbye after ten years? Indeed I was very grateful, but that didn't make the job satisfying.

I had been invited many times to visit with the executive director of the Loft Literary Center, who wanted W^3 to partner with them on one program or another. I always declined, fearing that what I had worked so hard to build would be co-opted by that large, internationally recognized organization whose reach was so much broader than mine. Also, their reputation was that they catered mostly to white writers with means and swallowed up smaller efforts to accommodate writers who were not in their primary demographic. But one day I learned that their program director was leaving.

Despite my misgivings, I saw an opportunity to return to the arts. I decided to apply and was hired. For the next five years, from 1989 till 1993, I was able to build on what I had learned in the arts administration classes Lawrence had sent me to. I learned much more about directing programs and the many aspects of running an arts organization that was much larger than W³ had been. But it was not without difficulties.

I was the first person of color to hold a leadership position at the Loft. As is so often true, the problem with being the first is that you are invited into an existing structure where others do not know or understand that our way of being is different from theirs. It was a constant struggle. My views and opinions were constantly questioned or outright dismissed as unacceptable or invalid. In addition, I felt pigeonholed by their members. As program director, I was responsible for their signature programs as well as Inroads, the new program they had started for indigenous writers and writers of color just before I was hired. Yet during my entire time there, I often heard comments from constituents that showed they thought that my job was only to manage Inroads—no matter how many times I stood at the podium to introduce featured authors or winners of competitions. It became clear early in my tenure there that my values were very different from theirs.

I left nearly every day feeling hurt, humiliated, and

angry because of things that were said or done to me. But at the same time, I had developed a deep fondness for many of the writers I met or worked with. I didn't want to leave them or the position that had given me a certain amount of prestige in the community of writers. Also, Tania and Ebony were still living at home. I didn't want to take a chance on taking them back to poverty.

Over time, the stress began to wear me down. The final straw happened when I brought in a well-known author for what was then a month-long creative nonfiction mentorship. Within the first week of his visit, I became very ill and was diagnosed with viral meningitis. The writer called me at home after learning that I was going to be out for a while. I don't remember his words exactly but the gist was something like this: "I've been watching how they treat you. They've made you sick. Don't let them kill you." The illness forced me to miss my first granddaughter's birth the same week. Enough is enough, I thought, and submitted my letter of resignation.

The director asked me stay on part-time for six months so she could figure out who might be the right person to replace me. I didn't have another job lined up so I agreed. As word spread throughout the community that I was leaving, I started receiving calls and emails from writers, some who had participated in W^3 programs, suggesting that I start another organization to expand opportunities for Minnesota writers.

At first I was reluctant, but at the end of the six months I changed my mind. I called my friend Fred Meyer, founder of Ideas To Go, an innovation process consulting firm where I sometimes worked as a Creative Consumer®. He volunteered to lead an ideation session using his principle of "forness" rather than "againstness," to help the participants focus on brainstorming what a new organization for writers would look like rather than wasting time complaining about what we felt was lacking in the literary community. Eighteen writers showed up—a diverse group in terms of race, age, sexual orientation, experience, and genre, and the result was that a new organization would fully embrace my values. It would be based in a small office and would engage in multiple collaborations, taking its programming out to the community rather than asking everyone to come to us. In this way, we could keep it accessible to individuals at a wide range of income and experience levels.

We named the new organization SASE: The Write Place and playfully called it *Sassy*. The name was intended to be a play on the S.A.S.E. (self-addressed, stamped envelope). All artists know to include a SASE with submissions for grants and publications. If your SASE is returned, it means you didn't get what you had applied for. We joked that our name was a twist on that concept: at Sassy, everybody won.

A week after the meeting with Meyer, one of my neighbors saw the name of W^3 in the Unclaimed Properties section of the *Minneapolis Star Tribune*. I followed up and learned that a $1,000 donation had been waiting for us for five years. I used the funds for SASE's start-up costs, changing the name of the Whittier Writers' Workshop to SASE: The Write Place. We rented a small office in the 711 building on Lyndale Avenue and Lake Street in South Minneapolis, and we opened our door in fall 1993. I was fortunate that Minnesota's major arts funders, particularly the Jerome, McKnight, and St. Paul Travelers Foundations, and the Metropolitan Regional Arts Council (MRAC), remembered me from W^3 and the Loft and were eager to help get SASE off the ground.

We were able to start some of the programming envisioned in the ideation session immediately. Board member Julie Landsman arranged a meeting with the principal and social worker at Patrick Henry High School in North Minneapolis, which resulted in the Breakfast Club, named after the popular 1985 teen film. The school had a Saturday school program that gave students who had blown off detention all week a final opportunity to serve their detention on Saturday morning. The drawback was that the students had to sit in a room for four hours with nothing to do. SASE's Breakfast Club invited them to spend two of those hours in a separate room where they were given donuts, juice, and a poetry class. We hired poets to teach the classes and gave a neighborhood mother a stipend to keep order. The program became so popular that students returned even when they were not on detention. Word spread throughout the school, and more students began to attend. Then parents and other neighborhood residents started attending, and the community newspaper, *Camden News,* began publishing poems written by participants. This encouraged us to develop writing programs for teen parents in other high schools and interdisciplinary programs in partnership with social service agencies such as the Wilder Foundation and the Sexual Violence Center, where clients could explore issues they were contending with through writing and other arts mediums.

I was eager to pay things forward by using the gift Lawrence Hutera had given me. He had provided the impetus for me to start W^3 and had supported me every step of the way. I wanted to do the same thing at SASE, so I decided that if someone came to me with an idea, I would help them get it off the ground. Over time, our programs for practicing writers included exciting programs led by writers. The SASE About Town reading series, suggested by Brenda Bell Brown, became a place where writers could curate monthly readings in community gathering places of their own choice. Readings were held in coffee houses, libraries, and community centers, broadening opportunities for writers to share their work. With thanks to MRAC, we were the first program to regularly provide the curators and presenters with a small stipend. An unexpected benefit was that individuals who just happened to be on the premises during a reading often reported that they learned that writing wasn't something mysterious reserved only for a few lofty individuals: it is also for everyday people.

Writers kept coming to me with viable ideas, and those who were serious worked hard to put them into practice. Sherry Quan Lee started a mentoring program where small groups of emerging writers were mentored for a semester or longer, and e. g. bailey helped me start the Verve grants, the first grants in the nation for spoken word artists. Both programs were graciously funded by the Jerome Foundation, which also funded a small grants program that we called the SASE/Jerome Fellowships. Each year's winners selected finalists and then, by interviewing them, chose the next years' winners.

Diego Vazquez asked if SASE would consider sponsoring the National Poetry Slam (NPS). It took three years of going to NPS headquarters in Chicago before they finally agreed. During those three years, I became known as Slamgranny, a title I still embrace, though I rarely attend poetry slams anymore. Through the efforts of an amazing team led by Cynthia French, NPS 2000 was named the best National Poetry Slam at the time because we were so well organized. Sixty-five teams of poets from all over the country as well as one from Canada and another from England spent five days in Minneapolis. The competitions were held in venues in the North Loop, then known as the Warehouse District. Finals night was held at the State Theater and was opened with a ceremonial dance by a group of Aztec dancers.

Other programs I'm proud of were a curriculum we developed with Deaf poet Cara Barnett in collaboration with Metro Deaf School. Following that, we published a book written by poet and ASL interpreter Morgan Grayce Willow. *Crossing That Bridge* is intended to help arts organizations' efforts to provide interpretation for the Deaf.

I started teaching at Hamline University during my third year at SASE, and soon students began to intern with us. One of them, Brandon Lussier, eventually became our director of programs. A world traveler, Brandon visited a poetry library in Scotland one summer. When he returned, he wanted to start a poetry library in our small office. He recruited another intern to help him establish the library and to seek donations of poetry in all forms. Soon we had more than five thousand volumes—books, recordings, anthologies for adults and children. The Brandon Lussier Poetry Library was the only library in Minnesota dedicated solely to poetry.

MY INTENTION was to stay at SASE for five years and then to focus on my writing. But it kept growing in ways that were very satisfying. In our tenth year, I began to feel the signs of burnout. I wanted to move on but didn't know how. Eventually, I told trusted board members how I was feeling. To my surprise, they said they already knew. We had been having financial difficulties for a while, and one board member pointed out that when the leader is no longer engaged, it shows up in the organization's health.

Over the next few months we pondered what to do. SASE would still be my "baby," and demand was still strong and growing: our grants programs, and our classes and mentorships were still in demand, and mainstream and alternative schools, social service programs, juvenile justice programs, and other organizations serving youth and adults were still requesting our services. How could we free me up yet remain responsible to our constituents?

The St. Paul Foundation awarded us a grant to develop a transition plan led by Diane Espaldon of Larson Allen Weishair, and support from the Bush Foundation enabled us to strengthen our management structure by hiring a part-time executive director who we thought would eventually replace me. However, through our yearlong process of visioning and planning, it became clear that rather than bring in a new leader a merger might be the best way to accomplish what we were looking for. But who would be a merger partner that would respect our vision and further our programs?

I had been partnering with Intermedia Arts since my time at W³ and had a solid relationship with them. I approached Sandy Agustin, then Intermedia's interim executive/artistic director. She and Daniel Gumnit, who would become their next executive director, agreed. As their name suggests, Intermedia Arts engaged the community in multiple arts disciplines. But writing and spoken word were not among the programs they offered at the time. The merger would bring SASE financial stability and would add writing to Intermedia's programming. We continued our planning over the next year. Before the merger could be completed, we would need to retire a deficit we had acquired. We approached the McKnight Foundation, the

Jerome Foundation, and St. Paul Travelers and were happy and relieved when they agreed to support the merger.

On Thursday, June 8, 2006, we celebrated SASE at Intermedia with a mock wedding. Neal Cuthbert of the McKnight Foundation "officiated." Cynthia Gehrig, then president of the Jerome Foundation, Nancy Fushan of the Bush Foundation, and Mary Pickard, then president of St. Paul Travelers Foundation, each gave the "marriage" their blessing by reading a poem they loved. And then the audience erupted in a standing ovation when Neal read the first line of Shakespeare's Sonnet 116, "Let me not to the marriage of true minds admit impediments," as Daniel and I held hands, officially marrying SASE with Intermedia Arts.

Following the ceremony, SASE's board co-chairs, Shannon Kennedy and Leslie Wolfe, along with Intermedia's board chair introduced poets who performed. Then, like any other wedding, there was a reception with cake, food, and dancing.

I am grateful to Julie Bates-McGillis, whom we had hired to manage SASE's programs at Intermedia. For the next ten years, she took great care of our programs and always kept me informed about changes she was planning to make in order to take them to the next level. But her efforts as well as the efforts of other staff came to an abrupt halt in fall 2017 when Intermedia suddenly closed. Hamline University accepted our poetry library holdings, but unfortunately they were unable to provide a designated space for them in their library.

FOUR YEARS after SASE's merger with Intermedia Arts, I received another award that validated my service to

Minnesota's literary community, the Minnesota Book Awards Kay Sexton award, which is presented every year to an individual or an organization to recognize their long-standing dedication and outstanding work in fostering books, reading, and literary activity in Minnesota. My dear friend Sherry Quan Lee nominated me and recruited several others to write letters in support of her nomination. Like the YWCA Leader Lunch award, I represented another first. The Leader Lunch committee had created a new category in order to honor me. I was the first person of color to win the Kay Sexton award since the inception of the Minnesota Book Awards twenty-two years before, in 1988.

I invited my friend and mentor Andrea "Andy" Gilats, co-founder of the University of Minnesota's now-defunct Split Rock Arts Program, to introduce me. "It is vital to keep asking ourselves, 'Who will I be while I do what I do?'" she said. "Carolyn believes that if we see a need, we can work to meet it. Her instinctive, respectful practice of cultural entrepreneurism, her remarkable persistence, and her sheer joy in seeing others grow and thrive are lessons in living for us all. By consistently choosing affirmation, optimism, and progress over anger, complacency, and exclusion, Carolyn has created models for people and communities everywhere."

Then she said, "Carolyn has always brought her personal history to bear on her professional work, and the results have imprinted themselves on the literary arts in Minnesota." I listened to Andy's inspiring words, grateful to the friends who nominated me and the committee who had selected me. I looked at my beloved family who were sitting at my table with me—my mother, my children, and my grandchildren, and I nodded in agreement with Andy's words, grateful that this time they could share the moment with me. Indeed my personal history deeply informs my work.

MY EFFORTS to focus on my writing eventually had results. It took a while because during my thirteen years at SASE, my focus had been on keeping it going and growing. I wanted to become known as much as a writer as I had been for being someone who made things happen in the literary arts community. I knew I had accomplished my goal when I was awarded a Minnesota State Arts Board Artist Initiative grant in 2016.

Recipients of this grant are required to give a presentation in the community. Like the work I had been doing since I started W^3, I wanted to do something that would impact the community rather than simply giving a reading. Several years before I received the grant, I was invited to read at a local bookstore. I invited some of the women in my writing group, Twin Cities Black Women Writing, to read with me. During the Q&A section, an audience member expressed surprise that we were all "so different." I was appalled by her comment, yet fascinated. I know her to be a kind and caring woman, and I'm sure her comment was sincere and that what she said came from a belief that she shares with many other whites—a belief that lumps Black people together as though there is only one voice from which we speak, as though there is only one Black experience.

I decided to create a community experience that would address that issue. My relationship with the Loft has changed greatly in the years since I was employed there. The organization is much more open now than it was back then, and I enjoy my current relationship with the Loft. I teach classes there now and served as a mentor in its Mentor Series program, one of the programs I managed during my employment there.

Thanks to Bao Phi and Sherrie Fernandez-Williams, Loft program director and program manager, respectively, I was able to do something meaningful at the Loft for my community project. I developed a series of three panel discussions that featured Black women writers—the first was African American women, the second was women with Caribbean backgrounds, and a third featured women from East and West Africa. I was happily surprised by the community response: we filled the auditorium with each discussion.

The response showed me that once again I had created something of value, so I decided to continue the discussions. The next year, while I was talking with Sherrie Fernandez-Williams about Nigerian novelist Chimamanda Ngozi Adichie's powerful TED Talk "The Danger of a Single Story," in which she warns against fostering stereotypes by treating one story of a people as their only story, Sherrie suggested that I name my series *More Than a Single Story*. At the time of this writing the series is in its fifth year. We have had many discussions that feature writers from a variety of indigenous and of-color communities, and we have covered many themes. Author/activist David Mura has moderated discussions with men of color focused on issues of importance to them, and we have developed relationships with the Hennepin County Libraries, St. Paul Libraries, Wisdom Ways Center for Spirituality, and other venues where we hold our discussions.

6

REFLECTIONS ON TEACHING

Thank you for another great semester. What I love about your class is the environment you create, which is as comfortable as it is stimulating.

—Jacob Stoltz, student, Hamline University

On the Friday evening before Halloween in October 1984, I walked into the Whittier Park Community Center to pick up my work schedule. There were lots of ghoulish activities planned for kids and adults throughout the weekend, including *Very Scary Theater,* a writers' theater performance that we at the Whittier Writers' Workshop had developed as part of the park's Halloween fare.

The building was busy that Friday evening. Some kids were playing floor hockey in the multipurpose room, others were making masks in the art room, while still others were running up and down the hall laughing and screaming while a Friday night poetry workshop was going on in a smaller room. In the lounge area, the fireplace provided warmth and comfort to a group of elderly people who sat contentedly sipping hot cider, and children who sat at their feet with coloring books and crayons. And in the lobby, director Lawrence Hutera stood behind the counter doing paperwork and talking with Jimmie, the big, ponytailed man whose job was to keep order in the building.

I wondered how the elder citizens could be so content with so much chaos going on around them.

"Who are they?" I asked Lawrence.

"They're from the psychic church over on Lake Street. They meet here every week."

My interest was sparked and I decided to try to make conversation with them. I walked across the lobby's tiled floor toward the lounge, trying to figure out what to say. Small talk isn't easy for me. But as soon as I stepped into the carpeted lounge, one of the gentlemen greeted me.

"Ahh," he said, revealing a gap from a missing front tooth as he smiled kindly. "You're a teacher, aren't you?"

"Why, no," I replied. "I just manage the park's creative writing program."

"You are a teacher," he insisted in a heavy Swedish accent.

Sure that he hadn't heard me through all the noise, I repeated a little louder. "No, I just run the park's writing program."

"My dear, you are a teacher." I glanced at his friends who were all smiling with approval and nodding in agreement.

"Someday you'll see," said the man. Later, I learned that his name was Carlos, and that he had been one of the best-known psychics in the Twin Cities back in the 1950s and '60s.

SEVERAL YEARS LATER, in 1990, my friend Julie Landsman invited me to visit her high school class at the

Minnesota Center for Arts in Education. After hearing me read at a W³ event, she said she wanted me to speak to her students about the techniques I use to write dialogue. I wasn't comfortable talking about writing, having never done so before, but I was flattered that someone thought my writing was good enough to invite me to talk with their students—especially in a high school that specialized in the arts.

A week after my visit Julie sent thank-you notes from her students. To my surprise, most of the kids said that the writing I shared, the exercises I gave them, and my personality all combined to make me the best guest they'd had that year. Julie confirmed that the students truly felt that way.

A few years later, I agreed to teach a creative writing class at South High School's program for teen parents, but I didn't have any experience other than visits I had made to Julie's classrooms. Thankfully, she agreed to mentor me. She helped me develop a ten-week class and held frequent meetings with me, coaching me throughout.

The class was harder than I had anticipated. Most of the students weren't interested in writing. Their minds were on taking care of their babies and making it through school. But I found ways to get them interested in telling their stories, and in the process I learned that one of the most effective ways was to be open with them about my own life. That made me real to them and allowed them to share their stories with someone who understood them.

I taught the class for two years and, in the second year, added a class for students in another program designed for eleventh and twelfth graders who were on the verge of flunking out of school.

I learned two important things from my experience

at South High. First, I needed to be creative and flexible, and to listen to them honestly and intently. The second was that I loved teaching, and I wanted to do more of it.

THE YEAR AFTER I finished working with the students at South High, I was surprised when upon the recommendation of friends, Veena Deo, an English professor from Hamline University, invited me to participate in a panel discussion on Black women writers. I didn't want to disappoint the friends who had recommended me, so I agreed, knowing that my shyness and lack of confidence had kept me from being a good panelist in the past. Through discussions with Professor Deo, I was assured that a discussion about my personal experience of having had to create comfortable spaces for myself and other writers would be appropriate.

I prepared a presentation that centered on how I, as a single mother without much income, had created my own opportunities to learn writing skills. But when I got up to speak, I became tongue-tied and wasn't able to say nearly as much as I had planned. However, I said enough to cause Karyn Sproles, then-chair of the English department, to ask me what a private university like Hamline could have done to help a woman in my position. Without thinking, I blurted out, "You could give me a job!" She gave me her number and suggested that I call her.

Because of similar experiences, I expected that the call would result in an offer to pay me a small amount to speak to Hamline's faculty and administrators on how they could open their doors to low-income women. Instead, Professor Sproles gave me a creative writing course the next fall and helped me write a syllabus and prepare the course.

I began teaching creative writing at Hamline in the fall of 1997 and found that I love working with college students. Creative writing classes were not required, so unlike the students I worked with at South High, my students at Hamline took my classes because they wanted to.

The first course I taught at Hamline was challenging, and I was grateful to have Professor Sproles as a mentor. I had a great group of students that year and decided early on to be straightforward with them, letting them know they were my virgin college class. They responded positively and helped me by giving occasional feedback on how the class was going. This allowed me to revise the course as the semester moved along. The other person who helped was my middle daughter, Tania, who had graduated from Vassar College that spring. I asked her opinion about such things as what makes a good teacher, how much reading is too much, how much time should an instructor spend with individual students? Tania is both my toughest critic and my strongest supporter, so I knew her responses to my questions would be useful. Besides, her college experience was still fresh enough for her to remember which professors she thought were good and why.

I had raised my children in a communal atmosphere in which, while they all knew I was the parent, they also knew they were free to discuss whatever was going on in their lives freely and openly. I made a conscious effort to bring the same attitude to teaching. In her book *Teaching to Transgress,* bell hooks says, "As a classroom community, our capacity to generate excitement is deeply affected by our interest in one another, in hearing one another's voices, in recognizing one another's presence."

For a creative writing course to be successful, I believe both the students and the instructor need to be excited about learning and should also be interested in learning about each other's lives. In the first course I taught at Hamline, it was easy to create such an atmosphere. The class, "Writing about What Matters," was focused on writing memoir. The students who took the class were interested in creating short memoirs about something that had occurred in their personal lives. My disclosure that it was the first college course I had taught helped to create an atmosphere where the students and I could learn together. Indeed, as hooks also states in *Teaching to Transgress,* "Excitement [was] generated through collective effort."

Also that year, SASE was invited to start a reading series at Hamline. The Loft Literary Center, which had been holding a reading series there for a number of years, withdrew so they could bring all of their readings in-house. I replaced those readings with a series that featured a newly published author, a graduate student, and an undergraduate student. At the time, it was a real boon to the Hamline community, as students had the privilege of reading with a real author before a real audience. Since that time, a group of well-known poets and writers developed the creative writing programs at Hamline that are nationally known and respected; now all undergraduate- and graduate-level creative writing programs come under their umbrella. I am happy and proud to still be teaching one or two courses every year.

MY SECOND YEAR at Hamline was difficult. I had reluctantly allowed myself to be talked into teaching two courses fall semester: "Introduction to College Writing" and the memoir class I had taught the previous year. SASE had experienced an unexpected growth spurt and I needed to spend more time in the office. And because I had no previous experience in working with a large number of students, I was ill prepared for the time and energy it would take. I was surprised that the intro class went well. The memoir class was a disaster.

In *Teaching to Transgress,* hooks recalled a difficult class she once taught that mirrored that experience: "For reasons that I cannot explain, [the class] was full of 'resisting' students who did not want to learn new pedagogical processes, who did not want to be in a classroom that differed in any way from the norm. . . . And though they were not the majority, their spirit of rigid resistance seemed always to be more powerful than any will to intellectual openness and pleasure in learning."

There were two women in the class who couldn't accept my laid-back teaching style. Their idea of a good class was the traditional model: a professor who stands in front of the class and lectures, setting her/himself up as *the* authority. But the most rewarding writing classes I have taken have not been based on that model. I elected to teach writing the way it was taught to me—using a model where everyone knows the instructor is the authority but everyone, including the instructor, sits around a table and engages in writing and feedback. Again, from *Teaching to Transgress:* "Any classroom that employs a holistic model of learning will also be a place where teachers grow, and are empowered by the process."

The two women whined and complained and eventually began lobbying other class members in an attempt to force me to manage the class in a way that was comfortable for them. I was surprised and dismayed; neither of my mentors had warned me, nor did I expect that the classroom could become a battlefield. Professor Sproles had moved on to another college that year, leaving me in the hands of a new supervisor, Dr. Alice Moorhead. Because of my nontraditional background, I was a little afraid to talk with her, fearful that she would consider me unqualified, even though I had begun doctoral studies some years before. I was relieved by her understanding and support and surprised that she too had experienced difficult classes and difficult students. When I confided my worries about being ineffective, she replied, "All good teachers feel that way." I remain grateful for her support and guidance, her expert mentorship.

Because of the support of people like Julie Landsman, Dr. Sproles, and Dr. Moorhead, I learned that Carlos was right all those years ago: I am a pretty good teacher. At the time of this writing I have been teaching two to three courses per year at Hamline for nearly twenty-five years. I was the first adjunct professor to win the Exemplary Teacher award, which I won in 2014. I've learned to use my nontraditional background both to my advantage and the advantage of others. I have taught at a community college and a variety of community venues that range from the Loft Literary Center to leadership programs, to prison and detention programs, to programs for teen mothers, and to agencies that serve mothers who are experiencing unspeakable distresses. And I find myself frequently being called on to mentor young people in arts administration as well.

For me, teaching is about much more than being in the classroom. I have become convinced that it is about listening to the students and finding out what's important to them, and then helping them find a variety of ways to consider what they need to say and a variety of ways to figure out how to say it—rather than presenting myself as *the one who has the answers*.

Carlos passed away before his prediction manifested. I wish I could have thanked him.

7

EXPECTATIONS AND ASSUMPTIONS

Low expectations are the worst form of racism.

—Sally Rudel, former assistant principal,
South High School, Minneapolis

It's 7:30 on a chilly October morning. I'm writing in my journal and peering out the window. I love the early morning, especially in the fall when I can take in the remainder of the nighttime view and witness the spectacular autumn sunrise.

I live two and a half miles from downtown Minneapolis. However, the city skyline looks like it's right outside my window. On a clear night the skyscrapers remind me of sentinels standing guard over the University of Minnesota's imposing West Bank Office Building, which sits rooted firmly in the ground across the freeway, seemingly touching the distance from my place.

Panning slightly to the right, orange lights move in perfect synchronicity, like a chorus line, atop a silo high above the city. Each hoofer gets her moment onstage as the lights spell out "G-o-l-d M-e-d-a-l F-l-o-u-r," illuminating the old mill that has been converted to a museum to educate the public about Minneapolis's legendary flour industry.

Straight ahead a series of bridges mark the communities on the East and West Banks of the Mississippi River. On the first bridge, the Hennepin Avenue Bridge, an arc of green lights casts mysterious shadows over the next bridge, which crosses the river from Third Avenue. As my gaze moves in closer to my neighborhood, I see two rows of yellow lights slanting downward beneath the Stone Arch Bridge. They kiss the river and tip their hats, alerting night-floating barges of potential danger.

Just as the sun is about to make its appearance, caravans of yellow school buses cross the bridge directly in front of my window. One caravan crosses west to east, the other in the opposite direction. As I glance at the children bouncing around inside the buses, I wonder how many of them began their day with a nourishing breakfast and how many are waiting to get to school for free or reduced-price meals? How many were encouraged to do their homework last night? How many witnessed violence in their neighborhood or experienced it in their homes? How many children boarded the bus from a homeless shelter? How many homeless children will miss school today because their families couldn't find shelter last night? Where are the children who have run away from unbearable home environments? Have they found their way to safe places, alternative schools, perhaps? How many children on those buses are native English speakers? Which ones speak Ebonics as their mother tongue? Which children dreaded getting on the bus this morning, knowing they would have to face a bully? And who are the children who couldn't wait to get on the bus so they could harass a child whom they consider an easy mark? I wonder which children will be greeted this morning by a smiling teacher, happy to see them, and which ones will be greeted by teachers who will take the glint out of their eyes.

An hour ago, rush-hour traffic began to whiz by on the freeway. I wondered how many of the commuters were teachers on their way to school. How many of those teachers were driving into an urban school from a suburban area? Which ones were driving from one city neighborhood to another? Who among those teachers slept well last night and left home this morning with a full heart? How many fought with their partner or their children before leaving home this morning? How many are lonely? Which teachers are excited to be going to school this morning and will greet their students with a smile? And I wonder how many of those teachers want to know all they can about the children in their charge in order to more effectively help them learn. Which ones are discouraged? Which ones are frustrated because classroom size prevents them from giving students the attention they need and deserve? Which of the white teachers have allowed racism to color their perceptions of children of color? Which teachers with dark skin take the rage and powerlessness of internalized racism out on students who look like themselves or students from other communities of color? Which teachers are burned out on teaching?

Later, when it is time to go to the office, I will drive my sleek red Honda out onto the street. If I turn right and drive up to the Seven Corners area, I will see students and professors walking to and from classes at the University of Minnesota, actors and dancers going to work at one of the theaters in the district, and travelers coming and going from the Holiday Inn. If I keep driving I will see people from around the globe: Somali women, young and old, dressed in colorful hijab; Indians garbed in saris and turbans; people with Arabic, Asian, and African features, many of them students, many refugees. I wonder how many will be shunned today or denied something because of their accent or the way they look. I wonder how many of their children will be harassed at school, labeled as terrorists.

If instead I turn left onto the street that will take me to Mississippi River Parkway, the scenic drive that accompanies the river, I will see cars parked along the street, many with U of M stickers glued to their rear windshields. If I drive a half-block in that direction, I will pass a row of low-income housing units that are neatly hidden from the view of the campus.

Last Saturday afternoon, when I turned in that direction on my way to the supermarket, I saw three grungy-looking adolescents walk toward a man who was ambling toward his parked car, a thin white man dressed in jeans, a Lands' End vest covering a blue-and-gray-plaid flannel shirt, and a long ponytail swinging down the middle of his back. When he saw the youths, he picked up his pace, quickly unlocked his car, jumped in, and took off, leaving thick black exhaust from his tailpipe trailing behind and blurring his *Who Will Save the Children?* bumper sticker.

The youths moved back into the street and waved their arms, gesturing for me to stop. I rolled down my window and listened as the first young man, a hefty Latino youth, explained that the three friends were raising money for a field trip they wanted to attend with the neighborhood community center. The second, a tall, extremely handsome young man whose skin color and hair texture caused me to guess that one of his parents is Black and the other white, nodded in eager agreement. The third, a skinny blonde girl made the request for a five-dollar donation. "I don't have any cash right now," I responded and promised to stop back by when I was finished shopping. For the next few minutes, we enjoyed an animated conversation as they told me about their field trip and asked questions about my car and my long, silver dreadlocks.

I drove away feeling sad, because at such a young age those kids are already so accustomed to people turning their backs on them in fear, that it doesn't faze them, at least not outwardly. However, it's common knowledge that unless there are caring adults in their lives—at home, at school, at church, in their community—they are in danger of becoming the next generation's statistics. The two boys are in danger of becoming chemically dependent, spending much of their lives behind bars or meeting an early death, and the girl may join a class of children that America prefers not to acknowledge: inner-city white kids from low-income households who become teen parents, gang bangers, drug dealers, addicts, or worse.

FOR A NUMBER OF YEARS I served as one of SASE's writers-in-residence, visiting parenting classes for teen parents, primarily at South High School. Because most of the advertising I have seen about teen pregnancy prevention is directed to African American girls, my initial expectation was that I would use my personal experience as an African American teenage mother to encourage young Black moms. I was surprised that there were many white kids in the classes I visited. In one classroom I was also delighted to see young fathers participating side by side with their partners. It was refreshing to work with a teacher who acknowledged that the girls, white or Black, did not become pregnant by themselves.

The numbers of white youths involved in the teen parenting programs that I visited aroused my curiosity about the demographics of teen pregnancies. A search of the National Campaign to Prevent Teen Pregnancy's website reveals that while the rate of pregnancy among African American teens surpasses that of other races, the actual number of teen pregnancies reported in the United States in the year 2000 was 787,610. Of that number, 346,980 were white teens and 235,650 were African American. The remaining kids were listed as Latino. In that same year, Minnesota reported 5,580 white teen pregnancies and 1,400 African American. My surprise turned to anger and frustration when I returned to the site's homepage. In less than a minute, six photos of teen parents flashed. Two or three young parents were pictured in each photo, but five of the six photos featured Black kids.

I saw that Website in 2009. I recently took a look at www.HHS.gov to see if the numbers in Minnesota have changed. I learned that in 2016, there were 1,073 live births reported in non-Hispanic white communities, 396 in non-Hispanic Black communities, 156 in American Indian and Alaska Native communities, 189 in Asian and Pacific Islander communities, and 422 in Hispanic communities. Why is it that stereotypes are so ingrained, so pervasive that an organization can support the very misinformation that it disputes?

I DROVE SLOWLY up the river parkway remembering when my children were teenagers. We didn't live in a beautiful condominium back then, nor did I own a sporty red car. Our living conditions were as grim as the conditions I imagined the kids I had just left were living in. I was a divorced single mother struggling to feed five children while also trying to cope with what I now recognize as depression. I wanted to be a productive member of society, yet I also wanted to be a stay-at-home mom, an option that I could ill afford. But it was important to me that my face be the last one my children saw when they left for school in the morning and that I be there with snacks ready when they returned home after school. At the same time, I wanted to instill in my children a deep knowing that the poverty they were growing up in was not a life sentence, that they could have better lives as adults.

I resolved my dilemma in part by starting my home-based secretarial service and teaching my children the practical skills of typing and proofreading. In addition, I enlisted the services of Big Brothers/Big Sisters and Hospitality House, a faith-based youth-serving organization based in Minneapolis. I insisted that my children's Big Brothers and Big Sisters be African American so that they could see living examples of what they could become. My younger son, Julian, recently told me that having a Big Brother and being involved in the programs at Hospitality House were the major factors that helped him resist negative pressures from his peer group.

MORE THAN FIFTY YEARS AGO, in 1955, the film *Blackboard Jungle* was released. The story, based on a novel with the same title by Evan Hunter, revolves around Richard Dadier, an idealistic English teacher on his first job in an all-male high school in a big city. The school is plagued by gang violence, but the teacher finds himself surrounded by apathetic teachers and a principal who doesn't want to admit that the school has discipline problems. One of the film's stars is the magnificent actor Sidney Poitier, who plays the role of Gregory Miller, one of only five or six African American students in the school, and the only black actor in the film with a speaking part.

At the beginning of the film, none of Mr. Dadier's students likes their new teacher, including Gregory Miller and Artie West, a gloomy, morose, white gang leader who has uncanny control over the other class members who look up to him and fear him. However, Dadier soon notices that Miller is the most intelligent student in the school—and the least bitter. Miller doesn't get perturbed when his classmates call him "black boy" and make other derogatory remarks that make references to the very dark tone of his skin. During the course of the film, Dadier gradually wins Miller over, and by the end Miller becomes the teacher's sidekick, breaking up the gangs and bringing peace to the school. In many ways, the Gregory Miller character reminds me of Yoda—the all-wise, all-knowing, unflappable, and completely asexual Jedi master of *Star Wars*—except that he isn't green.

I was a student in the Minneapolis Public Schools in the 1950s and '60s, and even though I was a girl, my experience was nothing like what Gregory Miller experienced in *Blackboard Jungle.* Nor were the experiences of my male peers. When we were growing up, our south side Minneapolis neighborhood was undergoing the classic American transition: Blacks were moving into the neighborhood and whites were fleeing to the suburbs. Like Gregory Miller, I was one of a handful of Black students in the schools I attended. But unlike Miller, none of us was singled out as wise or brilliant leaders. In fact, the Black students were hardly noticed unless our skin was light or a teacher wanted to humiliate us.

I remember talking with a male friend, Archie Givens Jr., who related a story that is typical of what our generation experienced in the Minneapolis Public Schools: "I remember going to a college fair and feeling excited that I was going to have an opportunity to see what various colleges offered," he said. "But when we got there, a man from Goodyear Tire Company called all of the Black boys into a separate room, and instead of encouraging us to go to college he told us about the great careers we should consider in auto repair. I remember vividly how humiliating it was, first of all, to see the white kids watching as the Black boys were called to the side as though we were criminals, and then to be told that we weren't good enough to go to college."

It's a good thing Givens's family taught him to believe in the importance of books, education, and ideas. It's a good thing his parents instilled in him the kind of pride and confidence that encouraged him to believe in himself. He never doubted that he was qualified to do more with his life than repair cars. Today, he holds a master's degree in hospital administration and presides over both the Givens Foundation for African American Literature and the Givens Collection of African American Literature. Located at the University of Minnesota, the collection is one of the largest, most distinguished archives of its kind in the world.

WHEN I REACHED THE SUPERMARKET I parked my car, went in, grabbed a shopping cart, and began my stroll through the aisles. It was Saturday afternoon, so there were many young parents with children of all ages in tow. Some of the families were clearly enjoying their shopping trip, but there were other families who were struggling. The children were screaming and the parents were trying to quiet them or were threatening them.

As I watched the families, I tried to determine which of the children were successful in school. I remembered how confusing school was for me. Related to this idea, I hope teachers will learn two things from my experience. First, I encourage teachers to expect that the assumptions you make about your students are likely not correct: it is important that you understand that things aren't always the way they seem. The student who tends to act out, no matter their race or ethnicity, is more than likely suffering in ways they don't know how to express in positive ways. Second, I would ask you to know, and be okay with, the fact that you may never be the person to see the results of any good work you do with difficult students. Yet these students may be forever changed by your good work.

From elementary school until I dropped out in high school, my best grades were always in the language arts. Teachers seemed puzzled by my ability to switch back and forth between standard English in the classroom to what is now termed *Ebonics* when I was with my peers. But rather than praising me for my bilingual skills, my teachers tried to make me use standard English in all situations, and some tried to make me use my unfamiliar right hand to write with, giving me the message, in more ways than one, that I was not acceptable the way I was. To make matters worse, the same teachers who acknowledged my talent in the language arts led me to believe that I would be wasting my time if I considered becoming anything more than a low-level clerical worker.

In the 1950s and 1960s, our bilingualism was not honored by the people who held authority over our education. Unfortunately, that is still the case. As the African American linguist Lisa Delpit points out in her ground-breaking essay "No Kinda Sense," "Our language has always been a part of our very souls. When we are with our own, we revel in the rhythms and cadences of connection, in the 'sho nuf's' and 'what go roun' come roun's' and in the 'ain't nothin' like the real thing's.'" I was the same as most of my peers: we all spoke two languages, and our first language was not acknowledged or accepted by the people in authority.

By the time I reached my teens, the principal's office had become my second home. I fought with other students, talked back to teachers, and was often suspended from school. I believe that most people, both my peers and the adults in my life, saw me as selfish, lazy, and uncaring. In truth, I was a shy girl who had successfully constructed a believable image of female bravado in order to mask considerable emotional pain I was suffering because of my life conditions. The exception was my eighth grade English teacher, Miss Johnson, who seemed to understand that my negative behaviors coupled with my propensity for daydreaming masked a fertile, imaginative mind. Instead of punishing me, she encouraged me. Unfortunately, by the time she came into my life, a pattern had been set.

At the age of seventeen, I became a teenage mother and dropped out of school and, for the next thirty years, lived a chaotic life that included a failed marriage, single parenthood, and untreated depression with all of its ramifications. Yet Miss Johnson's encouragement stayed with me and eventually led me to pursue a career in the literary arts. I'm proud that my five children are living successful lives with impressive careers and strong, loving families.

Because memory isn't always accurate, I am aware

that the facts about my interactions with Miss Johnson may be different from what I remember. I may very well be romanticizing her. But there is no mistake about the emotional memory that has stayed under my skin since eighth grade.

There is no doubting the lasting power that teachers have in shaping children's lives, for good or for ill. It is very likely that if she is still living Miss Johnson forgot about me a long time ago. But even if she does remember me, she doesn't know that she saved my life. If I could find her today, I would tell her so. I would also tell her that I try to emulate her example with my own students.

As I walked through the supermarket that Saturday I hoped that twenty years from then the kids from the housing project will have a Miss Johnson stored in their memories. But my mind also floated back to the ponytailed man who turned his back on them, and I felt dismayed that after all of the work that has been done over the past three decades to try to erase racism and classism, they are still pervasive in American society. Not only in school but in most other parts of our lives, and often in subtle ways.

ONE YEAR I joined a weight loss program. I was impressed with the leader, who was a fabulous presenter. She mentioned that she was a teacher, and I thought her students were really blessed to have such a knowledgeable teacher who presents so clearly. At the end of each meeting, new members were invited to stay around for an orientation. I was the only new member the day I joined and listened intently and appreciatively as she briefly explained the program and answered my questions.

Two weeks later, a friend joined me. We had planned to go to the gym and work out afterward, so I stayed for her orientation. I was taken aback when the leader explained the program in detail to my friend, who is white. She even gave her handouts and recipes, saying that she gives those things to all new members. Did I miss something? I looked through everything I had collected since I started the program, but nowhere were the items that the leader claimed that she gives to all new members. When I mentioned that I hadn't received those handouts during my orientation, the leader looked at me blankly—a look that in retrospect I realized she had given me during my orientation. Her response was an offhanded: "Oh, I didn't give them to you?" She gave me the items as she continued the animated conversation she was having with my friend.

For the next few weeks I watched in horror as the leader subtly passed over the other two Black members of the group or gave them minimal attention. In my mind, those adults became the students of color who have to face this woman every day in her classroom, and my memory took me back to my own school years and to those of my children. It also caused me to think of my grandchildren, who are students in Twin Cities public schools now.

Memory took me back to my middle daughter Tania's junior year in high school. On conference night we moved from teacher to teacher, all with high praises for her academic achievements. At one point, we were waiting in line for a teacher who was having an especially long conference with another child's parents, when one of the school counselors, Chester McCoy, stopped to talk with us and complimented my daughter on her intelligence and her consistently high GPA.

"Where do you plan to go to college?" he asked. Mr. McCoy, a Black man, always showed great interest in the African American students.

"The U, I guess," Tania responded, referring to the University of Minnesota.

"Why don't you consider Vassar or Wellesley?" he asked, a sincere smile spreading across his face.

We hadn't started looking at colleges yet, but Tania had already expressed discomfort about going to the University of Minnesota, a very large school. Mr. McCoy's comment was just what we needed to hear. Tania and I looked at each other, and the decision was made in that instant. She would apply to smaller, more prestigious colleges as well as the U.

The morning after she received her letter of acceptance to Vassar College, Tania left for school excited to tell Mr. McCoy. But to my dismay, she came home that evening, shoulders slumped, as she tearfully recalled Mr. McCoy proudly announcing her acceptance to teachers and other counselors. One counselor, a white woman, started what seemed like a chain reaction of discouragement, assuring Tania that she was out of her league. "My daughter did just fine at the U," the counselor remarked in a condescending tone. Tania heard similar remarks from teachers, which caused her to doubt her abilities, causing me to have to spend a lot of time reassuring her.

Well, Tania did just fine at Vassar without the encouragement she should have received from her high school teachers. Later, she earned her MSW from the University of Minnesota, and today she loves her job as director of student life at PiM Arts High School, the Performing Institute of Minnesota.

IN HER BOOK *A White Teacher Talks about Race,* author Julie Landsman quotes a principal who once told her that within two weeks of arriving at this school, students can tell which teachers like them and which teachers do not: "They know exactly who will help them and exactly who will make them suffer, without assistance, through the credits necessary to graduate." Though Ms. Landsman was referring to the alternative school where she taught, that statement is true no matter the type of school a child is enrolled in. Kids know when they're being treated differently from other children, and it takes a powerful toll on their motivation to learn.

It is vitally important that teachers, no matter what their racial or ethnic background, be honest with themselves about how they feel about certain young people. My granddaughter, who attended a suburban school for the arts, observed that her fifth grade teacher consistently treated African American children differently from how she approached white kids. She spoke to them harshly and punished them for things the white kids got away with. At the same time, my eldest son experienced a discouraging school experience from a Black teacher at an alternative high school he attended where the student body was primarily African American. The teacher was extremely rigid, and it seemed that internalized racism caused her to convey a message through her behavior, that she was wasting her time and energy because "niggers like them" couldn't learn anyway.

A little honest self-reflection will inform a teacher about whether s/he feels differently about one group of kids to another. For most of us, myself included, taking a look at the parts of ourselves that we don't want to face can be uncomfortable. However, when you are responsible for children's lives, this kind of honesty is vitally important.

Finally, along with my five children and my eight

grandchildren, I urge teachers to have a sense of humor and to be flexible enough to understand that if a student's learning style is different from what you are comfortable with, they should not be rendered unteachable. I am constantly surprised by the number of students in my college freshman composition class who are convinced that they do not have the ability to write well. On closer investigation, it becomes clear that their fear of writing is based on discouragement they experienced from a teacher in elementary, middle, or high school.

When I finished shopping, I pushed my cart through the cashier's line and wrote a check for ten dollars over the amount. The cashier handed me my change, and I walked out of the supermarket, climbed into my car, and headed back down the parkway, hoping the three kids would still be there. There was a mixture of surprise and gratitude in their eyes when I put the money in the girl's hand. Their field trip was the next weekend. I hope that they had a great time.

8

HOW LONG DOES IT TAKE?

To speak about certain pains is also to remember them.
And in the act of remembering we are called to relive,
to know again much that we would suppress and forget.

—bell hooks, *Sisters of the Yam*

On a cold January evening in 1990, my daughter Iris came to visit with her three-month-old son. She was unusually quiet, almost withdrawn, so I asked if anything was wrong. "No, Mom, I'm fine," she replied. But as she answered, she clutched the baby to her breast, almost unnoticeably.

From across the kitchen table, I saw red marks on her neck. "What are you doing with all them hickies?" I asked. She just shrugged and looked down, embarrassed.

A couple of weeks later, I saw fresh marks. Iris's skin is smooth and creamy like chocolate pudding, and it was painful to see her beauty marred. The aching sensation I had the first time returned to the pit of my stomach, but again I ignored it.

The next time I saw her, she told me her milk had dried up. I couldn't help remembering that day twenty years ago when I took her to my breast. She had sucked hungrily, desperately, then turned away screaming as though she was in great pain. I walked her and cuddled her, then tried to nurse her again. I checked to see if her diaper needed changing, then tried once more. Finally, as a last resort I squeezed my nipples only to find that my milk had disappeared.

As I looked at my daughter now, I didn't want to—no, I refused—to pay attention to the thoughts that kept begging me to listen to what was going on in my mind.

That night I tossed and turned for a long time, recalling the hands of her own father, Bob, around my throat. I remembered him coming at me as I held Iris in my arms; she was so tiny, hadn't even begun to crawl yet. I remembered how I threw myself down on the bed face first, almost smothering her, to shield her from the blows that came down on me. And I remembered my doctor, who had been giving me Vitamin B injections, saying that stress was what had caused my milk to stop flowing.

I wanted to help but didn't know how to bring the subject up, afraid of what her answer might be if I asked the question. What mother wants to know that her daughter is suffering, that history is being repeated?

I left my ex-husband at the age of thirty and drove through the Great Smoky Mountains of North Carolina with a black eye, a broken jaw, and my kids huddled together in the back seat of the car to get back to the safety of Mama and Minnesota. I spent the next ten years in poverty, raising my children alone.

I thought I was showing my daughters that they didn't have to put up with abuse. I thought I was teaching them that going through tough economic times was better than living with danger. At the same time, I wanted my sons to know that if they don't treat their wives well, they would more than likely lose them.

SOME DAYS LATER, Iris came over for dinner with the baby and her boyfriend. Twice, when he tried to pick up his infant son, the baby screamed as though he were dying. I saw the tall young man's jaws tighten as he glared at my daughter, blaming her for the breach between him and his son. I called her into my room. "What is going on?" I asked. She wouldn't look at me, just sat there wringing her hands and looking down at the floor.

The next day she called me from a phone booth and begged me to come and get her. Her boyfriend had beaten her up, kicked her out of the apartment, and threatened to kill her if she tried to take the baby.

I called the cops, then rushed to meet her, my head pounding with the memory of Bob's abuse when he transferred it from me to our children. I wondered why the example I thought I had given my daughter hadn't taken hold, and why it is that each generation needs to learn its own lessons, no matter what parents try to pass on to them. Mostly, I was grateful that Iris only lived a few blocks away so she wouldn't have to wait long for me to get there.

I will never forget the sight of the girl who waited for me in front of the restaurant on the corner of Twenty-sixth and Lyndale. Anxious for the light to turn green, I watched as she stood alone shivering in the cold, her clothes torn, and her face bloody. Car after car drove by, and people walked past, glanced at her, and kept going. No one stopped to offer help. Years later, Tania would tell me that she learned in her college sociology class that there's a name for this phenomenon: *bystander apathy.*

While we waited for the police, my arms tightly around her, I thought back to that night in North Carolina when I stood in front of the magistrate's desk pleading for help, my face as bloody as my daughter's was now.

The balding man who sat like a stone behind his desk just shook his head.

"Sorry, girlie," he said, barely looking up from the papers on his desk. "Can't help you. Go on back home and be a good girl." I couldn't help wondering what it was that stood between him and my blood that stopped him from helping me. Had he beaten his wife before coming to work that night? Was her blood on his hands?

Finally, two police cars arrived and escorted Iris and me to the apartment to retrieve the baby. My heart thumped hard and my hands shook as I waited for the boy to obey their command to open the door. What if he had harmed the baby?

I'm sure those cops expected the door to be flung open by an angry young Black man, high on crack, probably pointing a gun at them. But when my grandson's father stood in the doorway, dressed in jeans and a dirty T-shirt, nervously raking his fingers through his pale blond hair and peered at them with defiant blue eyes, the cops cleared their throats and shuffled their feet. And I was relieved that he was holding the gurgling baby in the crook of his left arm as though nothing had happened.

The lead cop could hardly get the words out of his mouth to order the young man to turn the baby over to his mother. The boy pushed his glasses up onto the bridge of his freckled nose and declared, as he gave Iris the baby, "I don't know why she called you. This is her fault."

After we got home, Iris told me that the boy, the son of a wealthy Ohio family, had been holding her hostage with the threat that he would take the baby away from her if she ever tried to leave him.

"You wouldn't stand a chance," he taunted. "I'm a rich white guy and you're just a poor Black girl. All my father has to do is call one of his lawyers, and you'll never see that baby again."

It hadn't occurred to Iris to question his threats. She just assumed that whiteness plus money equals power, and that she had no choice but to stay.

In an effort to comfort and strengthen her, I reminded her of the meeting I had with the boy's father earlier in the year. Because his parents so strongly disapproved of becoming grandparents to a child of mixed blood, I suspected that he had come to Minneapolis to offer her money for an abortion. I knew she wanted the baby, so I told her to arrange for me to meet with him. She shouldn't have to face him alone.

"I wanted him to know," I reminded her now, "that even though we are Black and are not wealthy, you have a family who loves you and that I am a force to be reckoned with."

I never found out if my suspicions were correct; the issue never came up. Instead, we sat around a table in the restaurant at the Holiday Inn where the man was staying, a very odd foursome: Iris and her boyfriend gazing lovingly into each other's eyes while his father, a chunky nondescript man in a gray suit, sat next to me.

After a while, he reached into his pocket and pulled out three chunks of metal, each a different size, shape, and color. He became animated as he talked about his job as the international vice president of his company.

"This," he said, referring to the octagonal piece, "is a sample of a highly refined copper." His eyes shone like the metal as he played with it, turning it until it hit the right angle to reflect the dim light in the restaurant.

Stunned, I tried to bring the conversation back to the kids. I needed to broach the subject of the baby. All he said, though, was, "My son can't even take care of himself, let alone a baby," and quickly went on talking about his work, showing me the silver-colored piece.

"And here's a piece of stainless steel. You probably have knives made of this."

As he droned on about his carbon and titanium products, I looked from him to his son and wondered what kind of childhood the boy must have had if his father loves chunks of metal more than a human being.

During the weeks that Iris and the baby stayed with me, I convinced her that since the boyfriend had a police record and was addicted to crack, he would never be able to gain custody of the baby. For further assurance, she called the baby's pediatrician, who said she would testify, if necessary, that my daughter was a good mother.

I was disappointed but not surprised when his pleas and promises to change convinced her to go back. And of course it wasn't long before he picked up where he had left off. By this time, Iris was pregnant again, but the truth eventually sunk in. If she stayed with him, her life and her children's lives could be in danger. Finally, she left him for good.

She did an excellent job raising her two children as a single parent. Trent and Tess are in their late twenties now. Trent is studying to become a pilot and Tess was recently named one of fifteen "Up-and-Coming PR and Social Media Marketers to Watch." Unfortunately, their father was killed in a car accident. Iris made many efforts to connect with his parents while the children were growing up; she sent school pictures every year as well as birthday and Christmas cards. Her persistent endeavors paid off after their son's death: Trent and Tess now have good relations with their paternal grandparents and their father's siblings.

9

I WANT TO KNOW
MY NAME

*There must be stillness for the spirit to
enter.*

—Anonymous

I wish I could find George today, the guy who gave me
my first journal back around 1980. He would be pleased
by the stack of journals I've accumulated since that summer evening so long ago. I wonder what he would think
as he watched me progress through my journals, from a
low-income mother just trying to survive to a woman now
in my senior years who was named one of "100 People
to Watch in the Year 2000 and Beyond" because of my
work with Whittier Writers' Workshop and then SASE:
The Write Place; who became a college professor, earned
a PhD at the age of fifty-eight, and is still creating spaces
for writers to discuss big topics. I can almost see his smile
while I watch him in my imagination reading about the
adults my kids have become: Tania earning a master of
social work degree and following her dream of helping
mothers and children, some in situations similar to ours
while she was growing up; Julian and his wife, Debbie,
who built a house in the burbs to raise their three kids and

then, after successfully raising those kids, sold the house and moved to LA to return to college themselves, Julian to study music production and Deb architecture. George would be so impressed to see how Stevie has grown since his release from prison, driving a semi and making music while being a proud grandfather; Iris going back to college in her late forties to follow her own dream of being a park ranger; and Ebony, who was still in diapers when George moved, who owns her own hair salon and does hair and makeup for celebrities as well as everyday people. All of this would surely bring on that smile I remember so fondly. Yes, I think he would be as impressed as I am grateful for the way my life has changed since those days when we were neighbors living in the vermin-infested green fourplex where I raised my children.

It's 11:00 as I write this, New Year's Eve 2000. I watched the sun set hours ago and am now peering out at the arc of green lights on the Hennepin Avenue Bridge as they cast shadows over the stone arches of the bridge that bears that name. To my left the lights on the downtown skyscrapers compete for attention while to my right holiday lights twinkle from the windows at La Rive Condominiums. In an hour, fireworks will erupt from the shoreline underneath the Stone Arch Bridge, announcing the start of a new millennium.

I WONDER if I would have the courage to tell George about the discoveries I've made in my journals that haven't been so pleasant—the entries about alcohol and messy relationships. Surely he knew back then that I could have been a statistic. In fact, I almost was. Sixteen years ago I was far from seeing my way off of the welfare rolls. Judging from stories he told me about his own background, George knew how easy it is to get trapped in the cycle of poverty that so often consumes women and their children after divorce. It happened in his own family after his parents broke up.

I wonder what it is that allows some of us to eventually escape while many, even some with deep faith, never make it out of the cycle. Surely there are moments in everyone's life that can serve as turning points, even if you don't realize it at the time.

THE PHONE RINGS in the intermittent tones that let me know it's a long-distance call. Who could be calling at this hour? My caller ID reveals that it's my friend Sheila. It's past midnight in New York. She must be calling to wish me a Happy New Year.

"Happy New Year," she says in her Brooklyn Jewish accent.

"Happy New Year back atcha," I reply in Minnesota Black.

"What are you doing?" she asks. "You sound sort of distant."

I tell her about the triumphs I've noticed in my journals, and I tell her how puzzled I am about the disturbing themes that have come up over and over again in the writing, and how much it disturbs me that at this time in my life I still haven't conquered some of the issues that bother me.

"I guess that doesn't surprise me," she responds. We recall the parallels that have often surprised us in the years we've known each other.

"I can't help wondering where it all began," I muse. I

believe that some of my behaviors come from patterns that are very old. "Maybe if I could figure that out, I could have a more fulfilling life."

After a lengthy pause, she says, "Here's what I'm getting: I think it goes back to when you were a baby."

Perhaps the biggest thing that has allowed Sheila and me to be such close friends is that we both have the "gift of sight." We freely and frequently share visions with each other.

"I suggest you do a meditation that takes you back to the moment of your birth. That's where you will find the answer."

Usually things sink in rather slowly with me. But not this time. Right away Sheila's words seep into that part of my gut that knows when a truth has been spoken. And just as quickly I see a purplish haze saturate the room.

"Do it now," she says.

I thank her and hang up, then sit for a moment, soaking up the purple light. I move the journals over and get up to light the purple candle that sits on my altar on the window seat. I change the CD to one I use for meditation, then sit back down on my bed and look at the clock; it's 11:15. I turn off the light and assume the lotus position, and I am instantly transported back in time.

I feel my body writhing, trying to get out of a tight, watery place. I hear my mother scream and feel rubber-gloved hands gently lift me up.

"She's blue," says the doctor and does something to ensure that my heart will keep beating.

There are other people in the room. Some are taking orders from the doctor and others are just standing around. Tension turns to relief when I cry; the doctor's maneuver was successful. Yet some of the people still look puzzled. There is something covering my face. It is soft and feels watery. It is preventing me from seeing the people clearly. The doctor takes a tool of some sort and peels it off. The brightness of the room startles me.

The doctor hands me over to a nurse who lays me in a bed and proceeds to wash me. She sings "Rock-a-Bye Baby" while wrapping me in a blanket. She rocks me and her hands are comforting.

"Is she awake yet?" I hear the doctor ask, referring to my mother.

"Yes," a nurse replies. My father has come into the room and is sitting quietly beside the bed, holding my mother's hand.

The doctor pulls up a stool beside the bed where my mother lies and tells my parents, "You've just given birth to a fine baby girl."

I see Mother's smile as the nurse carries me toward the bed.

"There are a couple of problems," the doctor's voice has taken on an air of authority. "She's going to be fine, nothing to worry about," he continues, patting my mother's arm. "She has a heart murmur. Not unusual—she's going to be just fine."

The nurse places me in my mother's arms and my parents begin to examine me, checking to see if I have all of my fingers and toes. "She is the most beautiful baby I have ever seen," says my mother, commenting on my copper coloring. My mother and father exchange words about how my older brother and sister looked when they were born, and then my mother repeats, "She is absolutely the most beautiful, perfect baby I have ever seen."

"There's something else you may want to know," says the doctor, drawing my parents' attention back to himself.

"Part of the membrane from the water bag was cover-ing her face. We see that occasionally. It's nothing to worry about; we removed it and she's just fine."

A look that I can describe only as intense fear crosses my mother's face and soon takes over her whole being. She and my father both know what that means. In African-based cultures, it's called a veil, while in Celtic cultures it's a caul. Others say the baby was "born in the bag." But in all cultures that believe in superstitions or esoteric wisdom, it means the same thing: a child born with part of this mem-brane covering its face is said to have special powers; my mother thinks she's given birth to a voodoo child.

My mother stiffens and almost throws me to my fa-ther. I feel her rejection so strongly that somewhere be-tween the time I leave her arms and land in my father's, my soul gets caught in a space that feels like limbo.

A black-skinned, fatherly man dressed in an orange African robe decorated with gold, rust, and burnt-orange circles reaches out and catches me, pulling my soul from the space in limbo. He is a shaman. He holds me to his chest, smiling and talking to me, calming my fears. As soon as the shaman sees that I've stopped crying, he lifts me up toward the Sun and gives me a name that I can't hear.

CRACKLING LIGHTS accompanied by what sound like explosions jar me awake. It's almost midnight, and outside my window sparks shoot up from beneath the bridge; the fireworks are about to begin.

I am sweating, shaken to the core. No wonder I've never felt like my feet were touching the ground. All my life I've had the feeling that my body's been on Earth but my soul has been some other place. I want to go back into the trance and find the shaman. I want to know my name.

10

THE BANK ROBBERY

*Each of us is more than the worst thing
we've ever done.*

—Bryan Stevenson, founder of the
Equal Justice Initiative

*This piece was written in cooperation with my eldest son,
Steven Holbrook.*

On November 10, 2002, my eldest son was sentenced to ten years in the federal penitentiary. Ten years hard time in maximum security. This wasn't the first time Stevie was given a number to replace his name. He has spent most of his life behind bars, a short sentence here, a longer one there. But this time it was serious. This time my number-one son robbed a bank in a lily-white suburb of St. Paul, Minnesota, a blue-collar burb with a shamrock as its logo, a thirty-six-mile area fifteen miles south of the Twin Cities whose census data in the year 2000 reported a population of 14,619 white people with a smattering of Asians and Latinos and one or two Black folks for diversity; it's a community with a median income of $65,916 derived primarily from heavy industry—refineries, industrial waste plants, and the like.

A few years earlier, Stevie was feeling frustrated. "Mom," he complained, "nobody wants to give an ex-offender a decent job or rent him a decent apartment, especially if he's a felon." But my number-one son had held on tight, and to his surprise and my great pride, some good things started to happen for him, a series of firsts: he worked his way off parole for the first time since he was a teenager; he landed a job driving a semi—the job he had dreamed of since I bought him his first set of Hot Wheels when he was barely old enough to walk, the kind of job that allowed him to feel powerful as he guided a mighty rig across the highways of the U.S. of A. praising God for the beauty of the plains, the hills and mountains, the rivers and the oceans that he witnessed along the way.

For the first time in his life, my number-one son had the means to buy a brand-new car, and for the first time he was blessed with a child of his own.

But one morning when Stevie showed up for work, ready to hit the road, he was faced with the shocking news that the company had closed its doors, leaving all of its workers jobless and leaving him vulnerable, in danger of reverting back to his old patterns. Ex-offender/convicted felon seeks employment. Baby's mama screaming on him cuz the rent's late and baby needs shoes. Powerless. Ashamed to tell the shrink he didn't have the money for the meds that kept his bipolar disorder in check. Powerless. Ashamed to call his Narcotics Anonymous sponsor or anyone else, for that matter, including the Almighty, to ask for help.

Shame has amazing power. It can cause a person to turn something around so that it begins to look like what happened was your fault—like Stevie was to blame for the company's problems.

Shame.

Shame buried just beneath the epidermis, the top layer of his skin, ready to jump out and bite him in the ass at a moment's notice. Shame stored in his genetic memory, imbedded in his DNA. Shame that started when his great-great-great-grandparents were shackled and forced to walk through the Door of No Return, locked up on ships that carried them through the Middle Passage shitting and puking all over themselves and their relatives, friends, and neighbors chained close together like they were in a can of sardines, then stripped of their history, their identity, their language, their religion. Shame passed down to him through three or four generations of family members who suffered the pain and humiliation that started with slavery and mutated into deep anger and self-hatred, one of the far-reaching effects of the phenomenon that Dr. Joy DeGruy has coined *post-traumatic slave syndrome.* It's the kind of shame that has no place to go except to be visited upon those less powerful, like spouses and children. My mama praised me for having put an end to the child abuse that's been in our family for all of those generations, but by the time I learned how to show my children that I love them, it was too late for Stevie. Shame. Shame. Shame on you.

It only took a few weeks for the positive energy Stevie had built up over a few short years of living productively to dissipate. He began to spiral out of control, sinking into that familiar black hole of drugs and alcohol. And on November 20, 2001, two months and nine days after the attacks on the World Trade Center, a year and ten days before he was sentenced to the federal penitentiary, my number-one son imploded.

Dear Mom,

Donna threw me out and I was living in my truck
so I decided to head out to Denver. I liked it when I
lived there before but it wasn't the same this time. I

got with this beautiful hooker named Celeste and got stranded when she stole my SUV. I tracked down the guy who hooked me up with her and pressed him to tell me where she was. He took me to her place and I met her grandfather. I told him she stole my truck and he got upset, frustrated with his granddaughter, saying, "I don't know why she keeps doing this to me." The old man, Calvin, let me stay there for about a week, until the police found my truck in the impound lot. I didn't even recognize the signs that said I was once again reaching the bottom of my life . . . which is always the stop before prison.

I had no money at all, so I called my little bro and he sent me enough to get my car out and get back home. I promised to give him the money as soon as I got back to Minnesota. In fact, I asked him to pick up my unemployment check and hold it until I got back, which he did.

I called him when I was about six hours away and told him that I would be there around 3 or 4 in the morning. He stashed my check on his front porch so I could pick it up without disturbing his family.

I blazed into town around 4 a.m. Stopped off at my brother's and picked up my check from the hiding place on his porch, hit the freeway, and headed to the check cashing place on Lake Street and First Avenue. It should have taken me about a half hour to get from his place in the burbs but at that time in the morning, when there isn't much traffic, it only took half the time.

My plan was to cash the check and run back out to Julian's crib to give him the money I owed him. But I ended up at the crack house instead. My custom has always been to get my dope and then look for a woman. Not necessarily for the sex, it was more about the company. I found this pretty, petite little Chicana and for the next day and a half, we went bar hopping, went back and forth to the crack house, and holed up in a motel in South Minneapolis.

I don't know what it was about this girl that made me want to keep her. With street women, time's up when the money runs out so I was trying to use whatever brain cells I hadn't smoked up to figure out how to keep her from leaving. When we couldn't stay at the motel any longer, I pulled into a liquor store and stole a bottle of vodka.

We polished off the vodka in a matter of minutes and right about this time the edge was coming off of the dope. I asked her if she had ever robbed a bank. She said no, but she knew of a way to rob banks by computer. I really wasn't trying to hear that because I was one of those here and now type niggaz. I didn't have the patience for all of that long-term hustlin'.

It was Tuesday, right around noon, and we were getting hungry. I pulled into a Burger King knowing that all I had were some bad checks from my account that had been closed, so I went inside where I could write a check instead of tryin' to order something at the drive-up window.

When I came back out, the girl was gone. I guess all that talk about robbing banks scared her off. But by now I had been talking so much about robbing a bank that I convinced myself to do it. So I pulled into a convenience store and stole a pair of those dark, mirrored sunglasses so no one could tell what I was looking at, and then it was off to the bank.

The first bank I went to was crowded so I left. Jumped back into my truck and just sat in the parking lot for about 20 minutes. As I sat there, I saw where I was heading—back to prison. I thought about all that I had lost in just a matter of thirty days: a good job that I loved, my woman, and my little baby girl. I began to feel tears well up but, Mom, I can't cry—not one tear fell from my eye. It was almost like those bitter tears were backing up into my soul.

I was in Apple Valley, not far from Hastings where there's a detox center so I thought, "I'd better get to detox, that's the only thing I can do at this point." I pulled myself together, started up the Bravada, and headed off with full intentions of getting off the freeway in Hastings and droppin' at the detox center. But as I was rolling through Rosemount I caught a glimpse of a sign that said, "TCF Bank Grand Opening."

Very impulsively, I pulled into the parking lot, a Cub Foods supermarket with a TCF bank attached to it. I circled the building and found a place to park, then I wrote a note demanding money. I put on my shades and my baseball cap, which read Female Body Inspector (F.B.I.—how ironic), and went into the bank and scoped it out. One of the tellers stood out, she was so beautiful. So I walked in, half mesmerized by the beauty of her caramel-colored skin—her long, thick, black hair, and her honey-colored eyes—and half desperate for the money. I talked with her briefly and she told me that she was Persian. Then I slid her the note. I should have slid her my phone number instead and asked her for a date.

She looked at the note and then looked at me like she was confused, like she couldn't believe what was happening and then she nodded her head in agreement. When she opened the money drawer and began pulling out the cash, I noticed a slot in the drawer that was stacked with $100 bills. Little did I know that slot had the device that would change the next ten years of my life.

The Rosemount newspaper reported that Stevie "used a threatening note and the suggestion of a gun to walk out with an undisclosed amount of money." Witnesses helped identify him. "As he ran out of the bank he had shoved the money down his pants and a dye pack exploded, which attracted the attention of a number of people. One wrote down his license number."

I imagine Stevie dropping the bag of loot down the front of his pants and trying to walk fast to the Oldsmobile Bravada, the SUV he had purchased brand new just a few months before, when he was employed. I see him looking over his shoulder because he knows that a Black man stepping into a new car in small-town Minnesota will raise some eyebrows. I hear the dye pack explode. Pow! And I see this red substance cover the front of his pants as he climbs into the truck.

Listen. Do you hear the crowd? Can you see people spilling out of the building? Do you hear them yelling, "Catch him!" "Don't let him get away!" "Give me a piece of paper. Gotta get his license number."

And I see my number-one son peel out of the parking lot, out of his mind from the pain in his groin and the crack cocaine that gave him the guts to stop off in white town and rob the bank, his dark eyes shining with a mixture of sadness, wonder, and surprise, glazed and sparkling like stars in a clear sky on a summer night.

I imagine him taking his right hand off the steering wheel and reaching down to unfasten the holster where his cell phone is locked, lifting the phone, and dialing somebody's number, then parting the mustached lips that hide his perfect teeth. But before he can get the first word out, the dye pack starts to burn in his crotch, making the insides of his bones scream. He muffles the screams, recalling instead the confusion on the bank teller's face when she realized that the glassy-eyed Black man who stood on the other side of the bulletproof glass, the ginger-skinned desperado dressed in dark glasses, a baseball cap, tight jeans, and a brown leather jacket, stinking to high heaven because he'd been up smoking crack and drinking whiskey for three days and three nights, had slipped her a note commanding her to fork over the cash.

But he can't hold the screams back for long. He has to keep moving before the cops catch up with him, but where will he go? He has to get that bag of hot money out of his pants before the substance ruins his ability to father another child. He's trying to keep control of his ride while his crotch is burning so hard that he wonders if he has finally made it to that place where it's rumored that Satan makes his home. I imagine him digging his sweaty hand down where the Sun doesn't shine and coaxing the offending bag of cash away from his parched skin, a long, guttural moan barely making it past the Adam's apple on his thick, brown neck. And I imagine Julian, my younger son, who has built a happy, prosperous life with his wife and three children, feeling hurt, bewildered, and disappointed, wondering why his big brother ripped him off.

> I put the bundle of money on the passenger seat and
> when I picked it up again it was still smoldering,
> traces of the red dye had burned through the tan
> leather seats. I attempted to see what I could salvage
> from the bundle. Now picture this, Mom. Here I
> am blazing down a dirt road with my pants and
> underwear down around my ankles, kicking up a
> thick cloud of dust behind me and tossing all of the
> destroyed, banded bundles of money that I couldn't
> salvage out the window. Then it was off to Rochester
> where I had a delicious steak dinner and left the
> waitress a $20 tip.

I hooked up with my dope man when I got back into town. It was the Tuesday before Thanksgiving and I had promised him a month before that I would take him home to Detroit to see his mom for Thanksgiving. You know me, Mom. How could I refuse a request like that? He was just a 20-year-old kid. He called me "Unc" and I called him "Nephew." I spent $400 with him, then holed up in a hotel room close to his house smoking crack and tweaking so we could hit the road on Wednesday.

I was still on fire from the burn I got from the dye pack so I showed it to the kid on the way to Detroit. He asked me what had happened. He grimaced and then told me that I needed to put some peroxide and Neosporin cream on it so we stopped and got some. Sure started feeling better.

Soon as the youngster and I hit Wisconsin, my cell phone rang. I knew it was Donna. She asked where I was and I told her I was on my way to Detroit for Thanksgiving. She asked me to come back and spend it with her and the kids but all I could think was, "You got some nerve. You threw me out of the house. I've been sleeping in my truck and you didn't care when I was stranded in Denver for five days and now you want me to have Thanksgiving with you?"

I talked with her again while I was in Detroit, told her I'd be back at 6:00 on Saturday morning. I remember telling her that I was on my way to greatness (whatever that meant) and she started crying. It didn't dawn on me until later what her tears were about.

Anyway, we started back to Minneapolis on Friday night. The youngster was tired from all the rippin' and runnin' we'd been doing so I took the first leg of the trip. Mom, I know you're familiar with Divine Intervention. Well, I believe that's what happened for the rest of the trip. God was not willing to let me go through with my plans for the next 24 hours.

I drove for about 4 hours and right around 6 a.m. as we were pressing through Gary, Indiana, and were about to head into Illinois, I got so groggy that I had no fight left in me, no energy. I turned the wheel over to the youngster and was about to nod off to sleep when Donna called again and asked where I was. I laid my seat back and went to sleep just as we were about to cross the Illinois/Wisconsin border.

About four hours later, the youngster woke me up in a panic."Unc! Unc!" he cried out. "We're getting pulled over!" Being a trucker, I knew how the troopers were in Wisconsin so I said, "Boy, I told you not to speed in Wisconsin." He assured me that he had set the cruise control at 60 m.p.h. so I told him to pull over and we'd straighten the whole thing out. But he said, "I don't think you understand. We are getting pulled over!!!!"

I flipped down the visor and opened the mirror and when I looked out the windshield, what I saw was like something you see only in movies. I swear, Mom, Wisconsin state troopers and federal marshals were everywhere. They had completely shut the highway down! You would have thought I was Osama Bin Laden, the way they came at me.

A few days later, as the marshals were transporting me to the Federal jail in Madison, Wisconsin, I naively asked, "What is a marshal? Is he like a deputy or something?" The marshal arrogantly replied, "Let me put it to you this way. I can go anywhere at any time and arrest anyone, including the President of the United States."

I thought, "Man, what have I gotten myself into?" Then I asked how they knew where I was. He said, "You guys all make the same stupid mistake. We know that if we really want you, all we have to do is hook up with your girl and she will lead us right to you." I learned very quickly what Donna's tears were about when I told her that I was on my way to greatness. She knew otherwise. She knew I was on my way to jail. And not only that—she knew that all the while she was working with the feds to catch me.

Something else I found out (speaking of God's intervention) was that if the police would have caught up with me 10 miles later, I would have ended up going to jail in a county of Wisconsin that is run by the Ku Klux Klan.

So here I am, Mom. 10 years for a bank robbery that I salvaged only $1,000 out of. That's $100 a year, less than 37¢ a day. Now that's crazy!

All my love,
Your #1 Son

IT'S NO SECRET that my son is one man among the enormous number of Black men in the prison system. I am incredibly grateful that he has managed to make it past the difficulties that made him vulnerable to the way of life that landed him there. The scars may never be completely healed. But when he tells me now of the young men and women he is counseling through Bible study and the songs he composes, and when I see how hard he has worked to make peace with his wife and daughter for the years they spent without him, and now when I see the pride he has in his granddaughter, I can't help feeling proud of him, and very, very relieved.

11

NEIGHBORHOOD WATCH

"If it hadn't been for that cup of cold coffee,
none of this would have happened."

—Allan Kornblum, founder,
Coffee House Press

I woke up at 5:00 this morning to the sound of a motor droning outside my bedroom window and flashing red and white lights reflecting along the wall. I got up and looked out the window and saw a fire truck, an ambulance, and four police cars parked across the street, blocking the entrance to the alley.

I threw on my bathrobe over my nightgown and ran down the stairs and stepped out into the cold Minneapolis morning. It was still dark out. Across the street, two newsmen talked softly as they pulled their cameras out of their vans. I walked toward them and stood out of sight, hoping I could hear what they were saying. But their voices were too low, so I walked directly up to them.

"What happened?" I asked.

"There's a dead man in the alley, ma'am," the younger one replied. I was stunned, even though I had guessed already that there'd been a murder. Why else would so many cops, firemen, paramedics, and reporters be here so early in the morning? Why else would they have draped the yellow ribbon that warned *Police Line Do Not Cross* between the leafless maple tree and the telephone pole that stood proudly at the entrance to the alley?

A crowd began to gather. Elders, young people, and children poured out of the old Victorian homes and '60s-style apartments that characterize the neighborhood. They were oblivious, it seemed, to the cold air, the early morning blackness, and the drizzling rain mixed with snow as they stared down the alley, past the yellow ribbon, to the bloody body that lay several feet ahead.

"I need to see his face," I muttered to no one in particular. I was desperate to see if he was someone I knew, perhaps one of the kids for whom my home had been a haven when my children were growing up.

I eased my way to the outskirts of the crowd and stood like a statue until I was sure no one was watching me. The cops were preoccupied, trying to keep order in the crowd of onlookers that was growing larger and more unruly. Then I took a deep breath, looked over my shoulder, and walked slowly toward the body, hoping to get close enough to get a good look before they pulled the sheet up over his face.

A deep sadness came over me as I looked at the still figure of a young Black man whose face I did not recognize. He couldn't have been more than nineteen, maybe twenty years old. And if he hadn't been so well dressed, his clothes so clean, except for the blood, I might have mistaken him for a homeless person who had found a spot to lay his head for the night.

He was lying face up. His LA Raiders cap, soaked in blood, lay inches away from his head. The stiff fingers on his right hand were frozen around a McDonald's paper cup as though he'd been struggling to hold on to it, and cold coffee spilled over his hand and onto the concrete.

When I looked up I noticed that my neighbor, Lynn, was standing next to me. I took her hand and, together, we began to weep. We wept for the boy's mother and for the mothers of the children who died in wars. We wept for the mothers of the boys whose bones were found in Jeffrey Dahmer's refrigerator. I guess we just mourned for all the mothers in America; the only place in the world where young Black men get blown away every day over a pair of sneakers, the wrong colors, or a cup of cold coffee.

We stood watch over the body until the coroner arrived and pronounced the young man dead, and took him away.

The next morning Lynn told me that, later that night, she filled a pail with water and went back out into the alley, got down on her hands and knees and scrubbed and scrubbed until all of the blood that the rain hadn't washed away was gone.

12

MY DAUGHTER, MYSELF

It is Friday afternoon, a crisp October day. I'm sitting at my desk looking at the clutter and thumbing through the message slips that have piled up through the week. I'm trying to determine which calls to return now and which can wait until Monday.

I go through the messages again, deciding to make a game of it, see who left the most messages and call that person back first. I sort through the pink slips, laying them in rows on top of the paper that clutters my desk.

There is a tie between three people who left three messages each. I sort once more, to find out which of the three called first. It is Maura Sanderson. She wins. I pick up the phone to call Maura, but before I can push the button to open a line, my phone rings.

"Hi, Mom." It is my thirteen-year-old daughter, Ebony. There's no school today. Usually I've heard from her three or four times by now on a school-out day, but this is the first time she's called today.

"Well, hi, how ya doin'?" I ask, brightening up.

"Fine," she says.

"Wuzzup?" I ask.

"Nuthin'," she replies after a pause. She is a naturally soft-spoken child, but her voice is even softer now.

"Well, whatcha doin'?"

"Nuthin'," she repeats.

"Is your road buddy still there?" Maybe Kyra, her best friend, who spent the night last night, has gone home and she's bored.

"Yeah, she's here."

I listen a little longer but she's still silent. "Is something wrong?"

"Yeah." I recognize fear in her voice and in her breathing.

"Do you want me to come home?"

She doesn't answer.

"What's the matter?"

Finally she says, "You know that boy Robert?"

"What boy Robert?"

"You know the boys that me and Elena and Kyra were talking to when you came home from work that day?"

"You mean the ones who took off on their bikes when they saw me drive up?"

"Yeah."

I'm sure she's going to tell me that Robert's been killed. I don't remember those boys all that well, and I certainly don't know which one was Robert. But I don't want to hear that another young Black man has been murdered.

"He came over," she says finally.

"Is he still there?"

"He didn't come over today."

"Well, okay. When did he come over?"

"A couple of weeks after school started."

I look down at my hand, aware that I'm still holding Maura's message. I put the pink slip down, place the receiver between my ear and my shoulder, and move my headwrap away from my ear so that I can hear her better.

"Where was I when he came over?"

"At work. It was right after school."

"Did he do something to you?"

I picture her curled up in her favorite corner of the sofa staring at the TV screen, her thick black eyebrows knit together in a slight frown, her worried look.

"Please tell me what happened!" I wipe my sweaty palms on my jeans and notice rings of perspiration forming under my armpits.

"Well . . . he . . ."

"Did he touch you?"

"Yeah."

"Did he . . . rape you?"

"Not exactly . . . well . . . kind of."

Suddenly, as though a light bulb has exploded in my head, I know exactly when it happened. I remember that day last month when I called her after school, when the phone rang and rang but she didn't answer. Nor did the answering machine pick up my call. I called back several times and was about to ask my neighbor to go over and check on her when she finally answered. She was in the bathroom, she said, and didn't hear the phone ring. I remember asking if something was wrong because her voice sounded like it does now. I woke her up, she said; she was taking a nap, she was tired.

I remember feeling a little suspicious because she never takes naps. But she had a busy summer, and now that she is in junior high she has to get up at 5:30 to catch the school bus on time. Besides, Tania, who always got home first, has gone away to college, and for the first time in her life Ebony is home alone after school every day.

"Why didn't you tell me about this sooner?" My voice is shaking along with my cold hands.

"You would be mad at me." A pang of sadness washes over me as I realize she didn't think she could trust me.

"What changed your mind?"

"We saw a movie in school, and my friend Peter asked me why I looked so sad. I told him about Robert and he said that if I didn't tell my parents he was going to tell them."

"What was it about the movie that made you feel so sad?"

"Well, it was about . . ."

"Was it one of those movies about date rape?"

Her silence is my answer. I tell her I'll be right home, and I hang up, thinking about how ironic it is that the person she has chosen to confide in is a boy. I am happy that she is aware that they're not all out to harm her.

I am preparing to leave when the phone rings again. It is an angry client who's been trying to reach me all week. I try to deal with her in a professional manner but am unable to pull it off. Finally, I tell her I have to go, I have an emergency at home. I promise to call her first thing next week, but I don't think she believes me.

I feel like I'm going crazy, but I manage to dial Ebony's father and reach his voice mail. His message seems to go on forever. "Some little motherfucker forced himself on our baby," I say to his answering machine.

I run out to the parking lot and am almost to my car before I remember that I forgot to tell anyone I was leaving. I rush back in to tell my supervisor.

"You've been taking too much time off lately," she said. "If you leave now it won't be good: I'll have to take measures."

I try to recall the last time I have taken any time off, but all I can think of are a few hours here and there for doctor's appointments, time easily made up by the frequent late nights and weekends that are part of my job.

"My daughter was raped, I have to go."

"Well, just remember this conversation," she says to my back as I make my way out the door and rush to my car.

Oh, I'll remember that conversation, all right. I'll remember being stunned that those words could be spoken by someone who was once a rape counselor.

The traffic moves slowly. Maybe that's good, I think. It will give me time to collect myself.

I breathe deeply, inhaling peace and exhaling love, trying to center myself, as I learned in meditation class. But a picture soon forms in my mind, a discarded memory.

It is 1957. I am thirteen and in junior high school. I'm about to leave the school building when Jesse walks up and puts his arm around my shoulder. He invites me to walk to the far side of the building with him. I've got a crush on Jesse and am flattered that he has finally noticed me. But when we get to the far side of the school building, four other boys are waiting . . .

A horn honks behind me, jerking me back to the present.

As I put the car into first gear and step on the gas, the smell of blood mixed with semen engulfs me. I will have nightmares for many nights and the odor will stay with me for months.

Home now, I take my daughter by the hand and lead her up the stairs to my bedroom, my sanctuary. Her friend, Kyra, follows close behind.

I take her in my arms, rocking her like I did when she was a baby, even though she will soon be taller than I am. I control the tears that lie trapped behind my eyelids and try to coax the story out of her. She pulls away and buries her soft, cinnamon-brown face in a pillow. I want her to know that I understand everything she is feeling: the shame, the guilt, the fear, the humiliation. So I tell her about the boys who raped me when I was thirteen. This is the first time I've talked about it since I told my mother and the doctor, who said I was lying. I am amazed now that Mom chose to believe that white man in the white coat, that she never questioned the truth told by the bloodstains in my panties. I had put it out of my mind until this moment, when I am forced to recall it as Ebony haltingly tells me her story.

She sees Robert and his friend walking by when she gets off the school bus. Robert says he's thirsty, wants to come home with her for a drink of water. "Oh, sure," she replied. Her mother has told her not to have boys over when no one is home, but what could be the harm in giving a thirsty friend a drink, for Christ's sake? Robert knows her sister has gone off to college and that her mother is at work. Nevertheless, he asks if anyone is home. She gives him a glass of water and now he wants to watch TV. She turns on the Black Entertainment Channel, goes upstairs to check the answering machine, then comes back and sits beside him to watch videos. She is thrilled when he places his arm around her shoulder; she's had a crush on him since early in the summer. She thinks his kiss is a friendly indication that he is about to leave, but she couldn't be more wrong. Before she knows what is happening, he throws her down on the floor and is unzipping her jeans. Fighting and screaming, she begins to cry and he lets her go. She runs upstairs and locks herself in the bathroom and tries to wash off his smell, trying to feel clean again.

The front door is open when she finally goes back downstairs. Robert stands in the doorway, seemingly contrite. He offers a weak apology, then adds, "But you know you wanted it." The next time she sees him she will not look at him and will refuse to speak to him. He will call her a ho and will place his arm around the white girl he is with and will walk away, saying over his shoulder, "A Black bitch ain't shit!"

MY DAUGHTER is lying on my bed and I am stroking her hair, which she hasn't bothered to comb today. I feel my eyes narrow and the nerve endings in my fingers become raw. I recall our phone conversation, hear her telling me she wasn't sure that Robert raped her. A rage builds up in me as I begin to realize that things haven't changed in the thirty-some years since I was raped.

There wasn't much back then to boost a colored girl's confidence and self-esteem, no matter how encouraging her family may have been. Commercials for toothpaste and Clearasil featured fresh-faced blondes, and Annette Funicello was the star of the Mickey Mouse Club. If a girl who looked like me showed up on TV at all, she was a background singer for some dude who acted like she wasn't there.

My children have seen the *After School Specials* and TV movies about date and acquaintance rape, but my daughter can't relate those movies to her situation. The fresh-faced white actresses who portray the victims are nothing like her.

And then there are those music videos, like the one I heard in the background when she called me at work today, where some young brother is rapping about a sister's big butt, or where young sisters with goofy expressions on their faces dance, sing, and shake their scantily clad little booties behind some dude who refers to them as *bitches* and *whores*. The message is as clear today as it was in the '50s. Rape don't be happening to no Black girls, uh-uh. We's bitches. We's ho's. We ask for it, we want it, we just be beggin' for it. We expect it!

Thirty-some years ago I was one of a small number of colored girls in my South Minneapolis high school class, passed over for dance line, flag line, the cheerleading squad, and the class play and was ignored as a possible candidate for student council. The thought of being homecoming queen was laughable at best. White boys flirted with us in private but turned their heads when they passed us in the hall. Colored boys sang, "Every time it rains, it rains pretty little white girls."

Later, when Malcolm, Angela, Stokely, Nikki, and their contemporaries called out for Black Pride, the brothers asked us to wait until they got their act together. We sisters, believing they would struggle beside us, waited patiently. Instead, the struggle gave the brothers license to reject us more openly, flaunting white women and leaving us to raise their children alone. To this day, some powerful Black men who embrace Blackness in every other way comment that having a Black woman by their side is akin to remaining in slavery. This attitude gives our sons and daughters, perhaps the whole country, the message that, as Robert told my girl, "A Black bitch ain't shit!" Is it any wonder that our young women have such serious self-esteem issues?

Her friend stands in the doorway to my room with a sad expression on her face. The phone rings and I ask Kyra to answer it. "It's your dad," she reports. I tell her about the message I left on her father's voice mail.

"Why did you tell my dad?" she demands, her dark eyes glaring at me angrily.

"I just thought he should know." He has been back in our lives for almost a year now, and I want to share everything with him.

"Aren't you going to talk to him?"

She shakes her head and lies back down.

"What happened to my baby girl?" There is pain in her father's voice as he wonders aloud why she won't talk to him. It was just a couple of weeks ago that he told me how happy he is that they had overcome his lengthy absence from her life.

WE ARE SITTING around the kitchen table like three statues. My daughter holds her head in her hands, her eyes cast downward. Her father is rooted in his chair, his 6'3" height and 230 pounds are so still that he doesn't appear to be breathing. He is an incredibly handsome man whose looks have improved with age. His skin is the color of freshly polished, fine-grained oak, and his intense eyes seem to peer right into your soul. His face bears the deceptively calm expression that was once a prelude to a night of violence and bloodshed in the streets. I know that later he will drive around for the better part of the night to avoid sleep and the inevitable nightmares about Vietnam that always recur during times of crisis. A week has passed since I got that call at work. We dealt with the police and the gynecologist, who assured us that our daughter is not pregnant and has not contracted the AIDS virus. We've also had a session with a therapist, who will work with both my daughter and me to try to help us sort this stuff out.

I have a feeling this story is just beginning.

13

SEX AND THE SINGLE GRANDMA

We delight in the beauty of the butterfly,
but rarely admit the changes it has gone
through to achieve that beauty.

—Maya Angelou

W̲ay back in 1962, Helen Gurley Brown wrote a book of advice for single women, encouraging them to become financially independent and to experience sexual relationships before or without marriage. *Sex and the Single Girl* was seen by some as a precursor to the Women's Lib movement, but many women vehemently dispute that view, considering it pop culture rather than a valid contribution to the academic discourse on feminism. But I can tell you firsthand that the feminist articles and books published back then, such as Betty Friedan's *The Feminine Mystique* and the translation of Simone de Beauvoir's *The Second Sex,* meant nothing to colored girls coming of age in South Minneapolis.

Those books, which focused on the academics of feminism, were not written with the everyday woman in mind. But when my sister and I read *Sex and the Single Girl* shortly after it came out, we thought we had found the ticket out of the mold of tradition our mothers and grandmothers were locked into. True, the book didn't say anything about dark skin or kinky hair, but it was easy to transfer much of the author's advice to our lives.

I was in my late teens and had just become a young mother when *Sex and the Single Girl* came out, and unfortunately I was forced to place my infant son in foster care. I wanted more for him than the life of poverty that teen and single mothers tend to fall into. Gurley Brown said, "No one likes a poor girl. She's a drag!" Her warning caused me to believe that if I wore the right clothes and makeup and found the right job, I might attract a man of means, while maintaining a certain level of independence.

I used the fourteen months that Stevie was in foster care to work two part-time jobs and complete a secretarial course. The small paycheck and tips I earned cleaning rooms in a University Avenue motel allowed me to buy a couple of expensive dresses and pairs of stiletto heels so that I could look like the expert I had become at demonstrating a line of high-end cosmetics to rich white women and their friends in their large, well-furnished homes in Kenwood and Edina. They seemed to think it added to their prestige to have a pretty young colored girl showing them how to apply their makeup while another served tea and little sandwiches and their afternoon martinis. But it was hard not to notice that the hostesses almost always set me and my products up where my back faced their china cabinet, or that they closed their bedroom door if they escorted me to the bathroom before I left their home and threw a sidelong glance at my purse when I came out. I had no intention of ever walking away with anything I hadn't earned, but I knew better than to voice my indignation about these experiences. I enjoyed the work and I needed the money. I am equally certain that the hostesses never noticed the acknowledgment the maid and I shared, a brief nod and almost invisible eye rolls and shakes of our heads because of their antics.

By the time little Stevie came to live with me, my view of what was beautiful had changed. *Colored* had changed to *Black*—and Black had become beautiful. I had begun to feel pride in my naturalness, and I wanted to emulate Cicely Tyson, who had made the short, well-trimmed Afro famous when she starred with George C. Scott in a short-lived cops and robbers television series, *East Side/West Side.* I moved to the East Coast and put my secretarial skills to use, landing a good enough job to take care of myself and my son. I let my straightened hair revert to its natural state and traded in my form-fitting dresses and heels for sandals and flowing dresses and dashikis, fashions that combined traditional Africa with America.

I met my husband in Boston and quickly learned that Helen Gurley Brown had told only part of the story. Indeed, my husband's pockets were deeper than mine, but he was mean as a snake. His drug addiction eventually sunk us into the very poverty that I had feared. I was afraid to come home, sure that my family would shame me for having let my marriage fail. In my mother's world, the world of the 1950s, a failed marriage was always the woman's fault. If your husband beat you, it was because you baited him. If he didn't come home at night, it was because you "drove him into the arms of another woman." If he failed to put food on the table, well, that was somehow the woman's fault too. But after ten years of living in terror, I finally gave in and returned home to Mama and Minneapolis.

For the next few years I enjoyed a bond with a peer group of young single moms like myself. We got together a couple of times a week in each other's homes or at the neighborhood park so our kids could play together while we gossiped and talked about kids, exes, and our current loves—or the lack of romance in our lives. It was interesting to me that those women, from a variety of racial and economic backgrounds, told similar stories of how their involvements with Mr. Wrong had started and ended. Whether we sat around a picnic table at Whittier Park, at Linda's dining room table admiring old photos of her immigrant Norwegian grandparents, or on my back porch late at night with a bottle of wine welcoming a new woman into the group, the stories were the same: the violent husband, the exciting bad boy who took off when he found out she was pregnant, the passive woman who had suffered incest as a child, the woman who had been left behind after putting her husband through school.

When my kids reached adolescence, I decided it was time to start dating again. And because of stories I heard from my friends coupled with my own experiences, I began to think that maybe Helen Gurley Brown's book needed an update. *Sex and the Single Mom* would include two new chapters: one on child care for the dating mom and another on how to deal with children who don't think their mother should be dating.

IT WAS UNUSUAL to find all five of my teenagers at home at the same time. But if they knew I was going out, they would all magically appear shortly before my date was due to arrive. When he stepped into the apartment, the kids put him through awesome scrutiny, ten eyes looking him up and down with intense disapproval.

It was easy to tell what they thought of my companions. If they didn't like a guy, they would sit in stony silence, barely looking up from the TV. If they liked him, they went out of their way to insult him in order to run him off before they had a chance to get attached to him. Like the time I went out with Jim Stanke. After introducing him to the kids, I left him standing by the door and excused myself to take one last look in the mirror before we left. As I started back toward the living room, I caught a glimpse of Tania circling around him, hands on her hips. I stepped up my pace but I wasn't quick enough. I got to the room just in time to hear her say, "My mom said your name is Jim Stanke. Well I think your name is really Jim Stinky, cuz you stink. Pee-yew!"

"I'll talk to you later, young lady," I warned my child as I rushed Jim out the door to safety.

If I stayed out too late, the kids would wait up for me. My attempts to slip in quietly never succeeded, I was never spared their five-part chorus:

"Mom, where'd you find him?!"

"He's too tall!"

"He's too short!"

"Too skinny!"

"Too fat!"

"Too dark!"

"Too light!"

"He's white!"

Each verse ended with their voices in a unified chorus. "Ick!"

On the rare occasion when a man dared to face my brood a second time, my eldest, Stevie, would stand directly in front of him in battle stance—feet spread apart, youthful muscles flexed. Then lowering his deep voice several octaves, he would look at the poor guy as though he could see right through him. Then he would pop the question: "What are your intentions toward my mother?"

In an effort to avoid the constant threats and embarrassment, I started sneaking out to meet my dates just like I did when I was a teenager. I just didn't know what else to do. On the one hand, it didn't feel right to keep bringing strange men around my kids. But on the other hand, they were growing up and would soon be leaving home to pursue their own lives. It wasn't fair for them to expect me to spend the rest of my life alone.

I found the solution the morning after my second—and final—date with a very nice man with whom I had stayed out past the curfew my five young parents had issued. Motivated by guilt, I treated the kids to a big breakfast that featured everyone's favorite: scrambled eggs, hash browns, toast, and hot sausage for Stevie; Froot Loops for Ebony; French toast for Julian; and waffles topped with whipped cream for Tania. Still, they complained loudly, each child finding something wrong with what they saw on their plate. My oldest daughter, Iris, who had gone goth and changed her name to Athena, sat at the table, arms folded tightly across her chest and fixed me with a surly glare while her blueberry pancakes got cold. Finally, she said:

"I bet you think I'm a good girl when you're not home. Well, I'm not!"

Then the others chimed in:

"Me neither."

"I ain't either!"

"Right on!"

"Me too!" exclaimed sixteen-year-old Julian, adding that if I ever dared to get married again, he would leave home.

Their message was clear, but I refused to be intimidated. My thoughts turned to a recent conversation when they had been making fun of people who struggle with obesity. I remembered talking with them about prejudice and how unkind their attitudes were, explaining that it's because of such bigotry that our people have suffered for four hundred years.

As I looked around the table at each angry face, I suddenly knew what to do. I would use my children's bias against them. I stood up and walked to the head of the table and looked each of them in the eye one by one, then declared in a clear voice, full of authority:

"If y'all don't straighten up, I'm gonna marry a fat man."

The kitchen grew quiet as the kids stared at me in amazement. Then, one by one, they picked up their forks and dug in.

WE TWENTYSOMETHINGS of the 1960s are grandmothers now, and many of us are single again. I think it's time for another sequel. *Sex and the Single Grandma* will have three new chapters. One will be on how to deal with adult kids who still don't want to share your affection. The second will be on how to handle grandchildren who think you're too old to be dating. And the third will be on internet dating.

I joined the internet bandwagon after two of my friends met the loves of their aging lives that way. One of the great things about internet dating is that you can carry on a correspondence with a guy until you feel comfortable enough to meet him in person. It's almost like old-fashioned letter writing, except that sitting down with a pen, stationery, and a stamp was much cheaper than the monthly fees to the phone company, your internet provider, and the dating service.

I've avoided some potentially uncomfortable situations by dragging correspondence on for a while. Like the guy who sent me a chapter of his novel-in-progress after we'd been emailing for a few weeks. His protagonist, a Mr. George W. Bush, was chosen by God to save the world, and it turned out that the man was a self-appointed evangelizer, committed to using any venue he could find, even dating services, to win converts to the altar of Bush. Amen! Yecch!

Then there was the one who claimed frequent bouts of amnesia, leaving me to wonder if his claim was really a safety net in case he didn't like the women he met through the service, or if he was conveniently forgetting that he had a wife and children.

Not all of my internet dating experiences were weird. I developed an affectionate though short-lived friendship with an attractive Italian who didn't reveal any insanities or ulterior motives like so many of the white men who made it clear that they just wanted to see if it's different with a black woman.

After a couple of coffee and dinner dates and good conversations, I invited Mr. Italy over one Saturday evening. I tried to be subtle when telling my kids they didn't need to call or stop by that night. But apparently I wasn't subtle enough. Stevie has always been a master of timing. When he was a teenager, he always showed up at dinnertime, no matter where he was coming from or what time dinner was ready, and he showed up right on time that night. He gave Mr. Italy the requisite hate stare, glanced disgustedly at the wine glasses on the flower- and candle-laden table I had set, and then planted a scornful gaze at the black chiffon pajama suit I was wearing.

He moved toward my bedroom and asked me to follow. Once inside, he closed the door. "Mom, what are you doing? Who is that guy?" my inquisitor demanded, taking in the intoxicating music, red roses, and candles that surrounded my bed. I responded with a wily grin. *Wasn't it obvious what I was doing?* He touched the gauzy fabric of my low-cut tunic top and then said in a sincere tone, full of concern, "Why don't you dress like Granny?" My grin changed to a belly laugh as I imagined myself trying to pull off this mad seduction in one of my eighty-three-year-old mother's polyester pantsuits and sensible shoes. I assured my well-meaning son that I'd be just fine and sent him on his way.

The next day Mr. Italy and I decided to catch an afternoon movie at the Mall of America. We arrived early, having gotten the times mixed up, so we purchased our tickets and took off for a walk around the mall in order to kill time.

There we were, strolling along hand in hand, feeling all dewy and fresh when I looked up and saw my daughter and my two preadolescent grandkids walking toward us. I panicked and let go of Mr. Italy's hand, but it was too late—I was busted. Iris made an attempt to greet us warmly, but the suspicion in her eyes came through anyway. My grandson, who is taller than I am now, adopted a stance similar to that of his uncle, and before my daughter could stop him he said, "Grandma, aren't you a little old to be acting like this?"

Embarrassed, Iris attempted to shuffle the kids away, but I heard my granddaughter ask in a stage whisper, "Mom, do you think old people do . . . you know . . . that???"

Mr. Italy and I shared a knowing smile. If I could have answered my granddaughter, I would have told her some of the benefits of age and experience. I would have quoted Helen Gurley Brown one last time. I would have said, "Oh my foes and oh, my friends—the results."

14

SAY WHAT?

So that is how to create a single story, show a people as one thing, as only one thing, over and over again, and that is what they become.

—Chimamanda Ngozi Adichie

For years, I have heard compliments about my voice. People who participate in my journaling workshops frequently describe my voice as soothing, and they tell me it makes them feel safe enough to reveal things they hadn't shared before. My college students often say my voice is warm yet authoritative. They tell me it makes them listen, even when I'm saying something that doesn't have much substance. Back in the 1980s my friend Carter called me "E. F. Holbrook," comparing my voice to the popular commercials about the E. F. Hutton brokerage firm. "When E. F. Hutton speaks, people listen," the voice-over proclaimed. I laughed, but clearly Carter heard what my students hear. And let's not forget the men who said my voice had put a spell on them. One of them joked that I could make a lot of money doing phone sex.

My children hear my voice in ways others are not privy to: the gentle tones, when they were little, that convinced them that the silly songs I sang out of tune would heal their owies; the shrill, scratchy tone that came out nearly unbidden when my anger exploded like thunder when they were teenagers; the authoritarian voice that left no doubt that I meant it when I said, "If y'all don't get yo nappy heads up in here, I'm gonna [fill in the blank]"; the icy tones that said they had disappointed me; the calm, reassuring voice they hear as adults when they're second-guessing themselves and need reassurance, and at those times when, as one of my daughters puts it, "Mom, I need you to talk me down off a cliff."

I have often wondered if I could earn extra income doing television and radio commercials, or narrating videos and audiobooks. Maybe I could be one of the first women to voice movie trailers. In 2006, after I completed a merger that blended SASE: The Write Place, the literary arts organization I founded with another arts organization, Intermedia Arts, I decided to find out. I had been using my voice to lead literary programs and to teach creative writing, composition, and journal writing for a number of years, and I thought this might be a good time to expand my world. My voice had already provided me with small opportunities: I had narrated a couple of short films for a neighbor.

Conversations with acquaintances who do this kind of work, coupled with a Google search, revealed that there are a good number of talent agencies in the Twin Cities, some that offer training in voice acting. When a friend recommended her high school buddy's father, an actor/teacher/talent agent, I decided to give him a call. I liked the way he described his workshops, and the price was definitely right. He said he was offering a three-weekend workshop for beginners that would start the following week, so I told him to sign me up.

The instructor's studio was in the basement of his

home, and he had instructed me to enter through the back door and go down the flight of stairs that led to the studio. My son Julian, who composes and produces urban hip-hop gospel music, also has a state-of-the-art studio in his basement and assured me that basement studios were not unusual. I arrived late the first day, the usual for me, and I was a little nervous, expecting to be the only dark person in the room, also the usual. I drove through the middle-class suburban neighborhood slowly and looked at the little white, beige, and light-blue bungalows, hoping not to attract any attention. I parked in front of the man's house and walked around to the back with my head up and shoulders back, trying not to look out of place in case any of his neighbors were watching. I hesitated for a moment when I reached the back door, and when I didn't hear any sirens I assumed that no one had called 911 to report a strange black woman lurking around the house. Then I opened the door and started gingerly down the stairs, hands sweating as I held on to the railing and took in the musty basement smell. When I reached the bottom of the stairs and turned into the room where the class was being held, I was relieved by the warm welcome I received from the instructor and the other students, all of them white, as I had expected. A thirtyish blonde woman dressed in denim cutoffs and a T-shirt flashed a bright smile and patted the empty seat next to her on the old sofa where she sat in the dimly lit room.

Just like Julian's basement studio, this one was equipped with professional microphones, mic stands, music stands, sound equipment, and a computer. Cables were neatly taped to the worn shag carpet, presumably to prevent injuries to clumsy people like me who might trip over them.

I could tell right away that the workshop was going

to be well worth the time, energy, and money I had expended to be there. The man clearly knew his stuff. The other participants were friendly and, like me, were eager to find out if their voices had the potential to be successful in this type of work. The man's teaching style was an effective blend of lecture and demonstration. He invited students to ask questions whenever they came up and he took the time to give thorough responses. And though his personality was a bit curmudgeonly, his occasional smile, a brief, flickering twinkle that flashed through the lenses of his horn-rimmed glasses rather than from upturned lips, showed that he enjoyed sharing his knowledge.

Much of the workshop time was spent with students taking turns at the mic reading from scripts the instructor had placed on a music stand and receiving his feedback on the power, resonance, and overall quality of our voices. Indeed, I tripped over the cables on the floor when it was my turn. And then, in keeping with my innate clumsiness, I spilled the papers from the music stand onto the floor while rifling through them to decide what to read. When I picked them up, a script for a Progresso soup commercial was on top. I decided to read that one and save myself any further embarrassment.

I don't remember the exact words, but the script went something like this: "We love your Weight Watchers–endorsed soups. My husband looks the way he did twenty years ago."

The teacher instructed me to read it again several times, each time giving me tips on how to make my voice more effective.

"Breathe from your diaphragm," he ordered. Then, "Say it like you mean it. Remember how your husband looked twenty years ago!" His voice was an interesting blend of Marlon Brando Godfather raspiness tinged with a touch of gentle matter-of-factness, a voice that perfectly matched his personality. My smiling classmates applauded, and I felt relieved when he finally declared, "There. Now I believe you. Now I wanna buy that soup."

Three weekends later, when the workshop was over, I felt pretty confident that what I had been hearing all those years was true: that indeed I had the potential to be a voice actor. My next step would be to make a recording of my voice and send it off to talent agencies. My son agreed to make my CD and to record his own voice as well, since he too had an interest in this work.

I spent the next few weeks standing in front of my bathroom mirror reading ad copy, stories, poems, and newspaper articles aloud, practicing breathing from my diaphragm and projecting my voice and imitating voices I heard on commercials. I smiled when Julian called one day and asked, "Mom, are you ready yet?" Though he was in his thirties, the call took me back to his childhood, reminding me of every small child's query: "Are we there yet?"

THE INSTRUCTOR promised to keep us informed about opportunities and auditions whenever they came up, and true to his word he started sending frequent emails. One of them, a commercial for a wet mop, caught my attention. I responded with an email expressing my interest and letting him know that I hadn't yet recorded my CD. He said not to worry: he would be doing the auditions himself, over the phone. I wouldn't need to read the copy the company would be using for the commercial, he said, because at this point they were simply looking for the right voice. I could choose what I would read.

We scheduled the audition for the following week, and I intensified my bathroom mirror performances, happy with my new ability to breathe from my diaphragm and allow my naturally soft voice to project and exude more power. I read passages from Isabel Allende's memoir *Paula,* about the daughter she lost to a horrific illness. I've always been fascinated with her ability to seamlessly weave the political climate she left behind in her native Chile with whatever story she is telling in her novels and memoirs. I read print ads that attracted me either because they were great ads or because they were so sexist that they disgusted me, in the latter case hoping to achieve a voice that warned, "Ladies, if you buy the line of crap this company is selling, you will be demeaning yourself and the rest of womanhood." And I read poems and song lyrics until, standing before the mirror projecting my voice fully, I decided what to read: the great Nikki Giovanni's poem "Ego Tripping (there may be a reason why)" always makes me stand up straighter, confident in my own strength, power, and beauty, despite the way America portrays me and my sisters, daughters, and granddaughters.

The night before the audition I kept waking up and looking at the clock for fear that I would oversleep and miss it, even though the audition wasn't until 10:00 and I never sleep past 6:00. I got up a couple of times and practiced. Then for the entire hour before the appointed time, I stood in front of the desk in my home office watching the Mississippi River flow past my window while I practiced breathing properly and projecting my voice, all the while praying that my fatigue wouldn't come through.

Finally, it was 10:00. I took a deep breath, picked up the phone, and dialed the instructor's number. He greeted me warmly and explained his process for doing phone auditions, saying that he would record my voice using equipment that would make me sound like I was live in his studio. He told me to read as though I was standing in front of one of his microphones, took me through a brief sound check, and then said he would cue me when it was time to begin. I took another deep breath and on his cue began.

"I was born in the congo," I read, feeling pride and power in my voice.

> I walked to the fertile crescent and built the sphinx
> I designed a pyramid so tough that a star
> > that only glows every one hundred years falls
> > into the center giving divine perfect light
> I am bad

I took another breath and continued:

> I sat on the throne
> > drinking nectar with allah
> I got hot and sent an ice age to europe
> > to cool my thirst
> My oldest daughter is nefertiti
> > the tears from my birth pains
> > created the nile
> I am a . . .

"Carolyn," the man interrupted. I thought I heard some urgency in his voice, but I ignored it and kept reading.

> . . . beautiful woman

"Carolyn," he repeated a little louder and with authority. I stopped reading. "Carolyn," he repeated a third time. "Take the Black out of it."

Did I hear him right?

"Take the Black out of it," he repeated. Yes, I had heard him right.

"Take. The. Black. Out of it!" he exclaimed a third time.

I STOOD IN A HEAVY SILENCE, my heart turning to stone from the weight of his words. I pictured the tall, skinny man sitting at his work station wearing the wrinkled white shirt, unbuttoned at the neck, that he had worn to all three of the workshop sessions, and in my mind I repeated the encouraging words he had uttered while critiquing me in his basement studio. I wanted to ask him, "Didn't you notice the Black in my voice when I read the scripts on your music stand?"

I wonder what his response would have been if I had asked him some of the questions that ran through my mind. What if I had asked him to give me a reason why I should take the Black out of my voice? "There may be a reason," Nikki Giovanni said. I'm guessing he would have stammered a bit and then replied that the company he was representing wanted a "traditional" voice. I wonder if he would have had the guts to tell me that the company didn't think the American public was ready for the multitude of voices that make up this nation today. I seriously doubt it. Instead, when I started reading, he had uttered the first words that came to his mind, the words that meant what he truly intended—uncensored, not coated with the processed sugar known as "Minnesota Nice."

I wish I had thought to ask him if he would be willing to take the Irish out of his voice, to negate his identity, but when I was finally able to speak, I couldn't find words. Truth is, the poem I read could have been written by any Black poet, past or present: Gwendolyn Brooks, Lucille Clifton, Audre Lorde, Maya Angelou, June Jordan.

She could have been a contemporary poet: maybe Natasha Trethewey, Elizabeth Alexander, Nikki Finney, Rita Dove. She could have been a local poet: Mary Moore Easter, Tish Jones, Sagirah Shahid, Sherrie Fernandez-Williams. Or it could have been a male poet. It didn't matter who the poet was: the man's reaction would have been the same. He probably would have seen any poem that spoke to strength or equality, one that offered a call for my people to rise up against the odds and be inspired to feel pride in who we are as a threat to his power.

As I stood at my window searching for words, my mind flashed on a scene from *Roots,* the powerful miniseries based on the historical novel that author Alex Haley wrote following the results of his search for his own roots. Every detail was clear as the scene unfolded in my mind's eye.

A crowd of slaves on a plantation in Annapolis, Maryland, watched in horror as a recaptured slave was brought for public punishment. Three white men on horses ordered two slave men to spread the younger man's arms and bind his wrists to each end of an iron bar. They then pulled the bar up with a rope and fit it into notches carved into two wooden posts that they had pounded into the ground. The young man screamed words in his native language, pleading for help from whatever gods he believed in.

One of the white men climbed off of his horse and handed a long leather whip to one of the slaves who had bound the runaway.

"Say your name!" the overseer commanded in a thick Irish accent, and then he repeated the words. Each command was followed by one or more lashes from the whip

and screams that made the slaves in the crowd wonder how much life the boy had left in his bones.

"My name is Kunta . . . Kunta Kinte," the young man replied in broken English, desperation threading through every syllable.

More lashes. "Your name is Toby," the overseer insisted.

"My name is Kunta Kinte," the young slave repeated, refusing to give in.

"When the master gives you something, you take it. He gave you the name Toby. It's a nice name, and it's gonna be yours till the day ye die." The man's tone was shockingly nonchalant.

"I . . . am . . . Kunta . . . Kinte," gasped the young man, trying with everything he had left to hold on to his identity.

"I want to hear you say your name. Your name is Toby," said the overseer and gestured for James to deliver more lashes.

Finally, when the young man had no reserves left, he said in a weak voice, "My . . . my name is Toby."

"Say it louder so they can all hear ye," said the man, pointing dismissively at the onlooking crowd of slaves.

"My name . . . my name . . . is Toby," gasped the young man.

"Aye," said the overseer. "That's a good nigger."

The women in their gunnysack dresses, their heads wrapped to hide their kinky hair, and the men in torn shirts and raggedy pants, all stared at the young man, their faces full of the grief of knowing that another one of them had had the Black beaten out of him.

AFTER A LONG SILENCE, I heard the man's voice coming through the phone.

"Carolyn. Carolyn. Are you there, Carolyn?"

"No," I whispered. I hung up the phone, then called my son and told him I wouldn't be making the voice CD for a while. "I don't think I'm ready yet."

15

EARTH ANGELS

Sometimes writing about a thing makes it easier to stand.

—Octavia E. Butler

As I sit in my car waiting for the light to change, I cringe when I see a bus coming up Lyndale. Whenever I close my eyes, I find myself back inside the moment when the dark-clad woman crashed onto the hood of my car, slid into the street, hit the pavement, bounced, then rolled into the gutter. It was two weeks ago, but still I can't stop my hands or my body from shaking whenever I draw close to that intersection. I wish I could find another way to get to my office, but even if I circle the block and take the next street over, I can't avoid it. Not really.

When the accident happened I felt like I was outside of my body, watching myself jump out of the car, leaving the door open and the engine running. It was almost as if I was someone else, watching me run over to where the woman was lying, someone else watching me tear my coat off and plop down onto the curb, and gently lay the woman's head in my lap and wrap my coat around her to keep her warm while we waited for the ambulance to arrive. She was so young, could have been one of my daughters. I wanted to keep her safe, like I hoped someone would take care of my daughter if any such circumstances arose.

People soon appeared, seemingly out of nowhere, some to see what had happened, others to help. A man in a dark-green hoodie and tan cargo shorts called 911. I wonder why I remember the details of what he had on but nothing about the woman who sat beside me and draped a blanket around my shoulders along with a comforting arm, or the man who gave me a flower or the person who turned off my car and handed me my keys.

A young officer with a blond crew cut took the police report. With a kindness in his voice that surprised me, he said he wasn't going to ticket me. "This is a dark corner and she was dressed in dark clothing," he said. "I probably wouldn't have seen her either."

An ambulance snaked through the crowd, its siren making those intermittent chirps that warn a crowd to make room so it can get through. While the EMTs strapped the woman to a backboard to place her inside of the ambulance, I asked if I could accompany her to the hospital. One of them replied that they could tell only relatives which hospital they were taking her to. And then as quickly as they arrived they took off, siren blaring, leaving me standing in the street watching the people disperse into the night.

For a moment, I wondered if I had been dreaming, but soon a middle-aged couple came over and helped me back into my coat. I had forgotten how chilly it was. It was March, and we were in that in-between stage where it might snow one day and you can wear a light jacket the next. I accepted their offer to take me home. The man helped me into my car and asked for directions, and the woman followed in their car.

Once at home, I rushed into the lobby and punched the elevator button several times, as though it might make it come faster. Of course it didn't, but when I finally got to my apartment, I rushed through the door and without putting my purse down or taking my coat off called Hennepin County Medical Center, Abbott Northwestern, North Memorial, and Methodist Hospitals. None would give me any information. One receptionist said, "Lady, we get a lot of accidents in here every night. Unless you can give me the victim's name, there's nothing I can tell you." I wanted to go to each hospital and demand that they tell me if she was there, but I knew it would be futile. I didn't know her name and doubted if I could describe her. So I sat on my couch in a daze instead. After a while, I fell into a brief, restless sleep and woke up screaming, "Something's gone terribly wrong!"

I COULDN'T STOP THINKING about the accident over the next few days. Couldn't stop talking about it either. I needed to know if the woman was all right. Friends and colleagues advised me to leave it alone. "She might sue you," they warned. But I couldn't leave it alone. My heart wouldn't be quiet. Neither would the nightmares and daytime images of her limp body sliding off the hood of my car.

Early in the morning three days later, the day the policeman said I could pick up a copy of the police report, I headed over to the precinct, which at that time was located at Twenty-fourth and Nicollet. I hesitated before going in, fighting flashbacks of a night some years before, when cops burst into my apartment looking for my son.

The digital clock on my nightstand showed 3:16 a.m., when I heard the hard, insistent knock. I jumped out of bed and ran to the door, sure that something horrible had happened. *A look through the peephole revealed three beefy cops, each with a hand on the butt of the gun in the holster resting against his hip. A fourth man stood in front of them. I assumed he was a detective: he was wearing a suit that reminded me of the cheap gray suits I see on detectives in movies and* Law and Order *episodes.*

I opened the door slightly, leaving the chain secure. My heart was pumping so hard that I could hear it. The detective, a short, slender man with graying brown hair, flashed his badge and asked if my son was home. "No," I replied. But before I could tell him that Stevie had called a couple of hours before and told me that he was in jail, having been mistaken for a guy who had committed a murder, the detective motioned to the others. They pushed past me and rushed into my apartment, snapping the chain on the lock.

"Wait, wait," I screamed. "Stevie's not here, he's in jail!" But by then they were storming through the apartment knocking my furniture over, scattering toys, and tearing covers off beds, yelling, "Where is he?! Where the hell is he?!"

My four children, who were much younger than eighteen-year-old Stevie, were disoriented from having been wakened so harshly. They ran through the apartment like scared rabbits, screaming their little hearts out while they watched the gang of burly white men in blue uniforms and guns rage through our home.

Trying to stay calm, I picked up my youngest and placed her on my hip and led the others who were clinging to me by then into my home office, my bare feet sloshing through a wet spot on the carpet where one of the girls had soiled her nightgown. I called the detective into the room, then picked up the phone, turned on the speaker op-

tion, and dialed the Minneapolis men's jail. I asked the man who answered if they were holding my son. The detective, clearly surprised by the response he heard from the other end of the phone, stopped his men. They left, leaving me to calm my children and to clean up the mess they had created. I never received an apology. Neither did Stevie.

I COULDN'T SHAKE the memory off completely but didn't have much choice but to move it aside so I could get the police report. I stepped cautiously into the precinct office and stood at the counter watching the blue-uniformed men and women, some talking on the phone, others sitting at worn gray-metal desks shuffling papers, until one of them, a white-haired man with a paunch, noticed me and granted my request.

Relieved that the police report showed that the woman was uninjured—just bruised and shaken—I rushed home, grateful that her name, address, and phone number were on the document. I picked up the phone and punched in her number, rubbing my sweaty palms on my jeans while her phone rang. Her answering machine confirmed that I had dialed the right number, the number for Cassandra, the name on the police report. My lips parted but the words I wanted to say stayed glued inside of my mouth. I quietly placed the receiver back in its cradle and tried again an hour later. This time she answered on the second ring. Fearing that she might think it was a prank and hang up if I didn't say something soon, I let my words tumble out, telling her who I was and why I was calling. I listened to her inhale and exhale on the other end, sure that she was going to slam the phone down and probably change her number. But after a moment she said, "I've been wondering how you're doing too." That was the last thing I expected to hear.

I PROBABLY SHOULD HAVE stayed home the night the accident happened. I hadn't been thinking clearly since my brother Ronnie had had his leg amputated two weeks before. But a dear friend was releasing a new chapbook that night, and I wanted to soak in the awesome power of her poems and the soothing quality of her voice, hoping that it would ease my sadness. I wasn't able to focus so I left early.

Thankfully, the reading was in the building where my office is located, in uptown Minneapolis's LynLake neighborhood, so I didn't have to think much about where I was going or finding my car after I left. I got into my car and circled the block and headed toward Twenty-eighth Street, pretty much on autopilot. I turned onto Twenty-eighth and was moving toward the left lane in order to turn onto Lyndale when a smell washed over me—that unmistakable odor of antiseptic mixed with the sweat of anxiety that pervades hospital waiting rooms everywhere, what family members exude when they are waiting for the outcome of their loved one's surgery. I tried to stay focused on driving, but the powerful smell took me back to the day of my brother's surgery.

THE DOCTOR came into the waiting room and reported that the surgery had gone well. Relieved, my mother, her best friend, and I were ushered into the recovery room. I watched Mama as she stood beside Ronnie's bed making small talk with the nurse who was tending to him. I've

Earth Angels

always admired my mother's ability to engage in small talk, something that I do not share. I was also deeply aware of the peace that had been growing between Mama and me over the past few years since my brother Woody and my sister Joanne had passed away. The tension that characterized our relationship since I was a little girl seemed to have disappeared in the face of these losses. And now that Ronnie was ill, I was grateful for the harmony we shared.

Once Ronnie was cleared to be moved to the room that would be his home for the next week, we walked a few steps behind the aide who was rolling his gurney through the hallways. We soon noticed that Ronnie was becoming agitated. Mama quickly moved to one side of him and I went to the other side. She reached over the side rail and rested her hand on his shoulder in an effort to comfort him, but he started tearing at the sheet as though he wanted to jump off of the gurney and run. The aide was strong and was able to contain him without much effort, and Mama, though horrified, spoke to him calmly, words I do not recall. But I don't think I will ever forget the desperate sound in my brother's voice when he cried out through a medicated stupor, "Something's gone wrong! Something's gone terribly wrong!" I gripped the side rail more tightly and watched my mother trying to hide the strain on her face. Her friend started praying, a prayer she continued all the way down the seemingly endless hallway until we reached his room.

Ronnie had been sick for years—first with schizophrenia and then with diabetes, which eventually caused his legs to be amputated. This would have been tragic under any circumstances, but Ronnie was a classically trained dancer and choreographer. He had studied with

165

the great Caribbean-born dancer/choreographer/anthro-
pologist Pearl Primus in New York in the 1960s. When
he returned to Minneapolis, he taught African dance and
drumming at the Way Opportunities Unlimited, Inc., a
center in North Minneapolis that had been designed with
a dual purpose: to help the city's Black residents feel pride
in themselves, and to diffuse tensions after rebellions had
broken out following the assassination of Dr. Martin Lu-
ther King Jr. He had founded his own dance company,
the Feast of the Circle Dancers and Drummers, and had
taken them to West Africa and Haiti to learn from the
masters and perform with them. And he had danced with
the Minnesota Dance Theater. A striking photograph
once hung in their lobby: a brilliant photographer had
snapped the shutter at the moment Ronnie reached the
peak of a powerful ballet leap, making it look as though
he were suspended in midair. I have always admired my
brother for his ability to accomplish so much with a serious mental illness. His left leg was amputated a year
ago, and he had been in a nursing home ever since. And
now his right leg had been amputated, slamming the door
shut and placing an exclamation point at the end of the
dream he had held on to for so long—of someday dancing
again.

ONCE RONNIE WAS SETTLED into his room, Mama and I
stood on either side of his bed, avoiding each other's gaze,
forgetting about her friend who had found a chair and sat
quietly out of the way. We both believed we needed to be
strong for each other, but in truth we were both as fragile
as glass that could be shattered at any moment. We both
feared that if we looked at each other, with even a small

glance, the tears that were pooling behind our eyelids would erupt.

The next day I sat beside my brother and watched him sleep; his skin, once the shade of black coffee, had turned ashen from the effects of the anesthesia, and his graying afro was in need of care. His deep, even breathing placed me in a kind of trance, easily enjoying childhood memories: memories of walking to school with my three siblings, all of us bundled up in parkas and woolen hats and scarves to shield us from the cold on winter days, or walking to St. Leonard's Catholic Church or Nicollet Park on hot summer mornings for day camp. Woody and Joanne, the older siblings, were charged with taking care of Ronnie and me while Mom did piecework at Honeywell or cleaned rich white women's homes during the day so she could afford to go to beauty school at night. Music played in my mind's ear with memories of us dancing around the house, Ronnie teaching me tap and ballet moves he learned at Billings & Betty dance school when we were nine or ten years old. Another memory almost made me laugh out loud: it was a hot summer day, and Joanne wanted to make peanut butter and jelly sandwiches for us to take to our summer program at Nicollet Park. She couldn't find the jelly, but there was Jell-O left over from the previous night's dessert. By lunchtime, the Jell-O had melted and our sandwiches were a soggy mess.

When we were teenagers, Ronnie studied and performed at the Moppet Players, which later became the Children's Theatre Company. One day he confided with a certain pride in his voice that the aging man who ran the theater wanted to be his boyfriend. I remember feeling horrified, not knowing what to do with this information. That night at dinner I looked around the table from Mama to Woody to Joanne to Barney, then back to Ronnie, who seemed all aglow. Would I spoil an enjoyable family moment if I said something? Would Ronnie feel betrayed? Would anyone even believe me? I decided to stay silent.

I sometimes wonder if Mom and Barney had any suspicions. I wondered even more after that man was publicly exposed years later and convicted of child sexual abuse. But that day in the hospital, the day after Ronnie's surgery, my most pressing thought while watching him sleep was that it may not be long before he might be my third and final sibling to go to their grave. And indeed, heart failure and complications from his diabetes took his life two years later. Knowing that he was gay, several of my well-meaning friends said in their offerings of sympathy, "I know what you're going through. I had another friend who died of AIDS." At first I was shocked, and then I was just plain pissed. Didn't these intelligent, caring people know that HIV/AIDS isn't the only cause of death for gay men?

AND NOW THIS WOMAN, whom I could have killed, said she had been wondering how I had been doing since the accident, continuing the pattern of kindness that so many people had shown me on the night of the accident. I wanted to tell her the truth, that I wasn't doing well, that I had lost two of my siblings over the past eight years and was probably on the verge of saying goodbye to the last one, my younger brother.

I cannot forget the night Joanne told me she was getting married. The call came a week or two after another when she said she was afraid of her fiancé. He had been verbally abusive in the year they had been dating, and now his behavior had taken a turn that made us both worry that his attacks could turn physical.

"Are you sure you want to marry this dude?" I asked, adding that I thought she should get rid of him, the sooner the better.

She thought for a moment, and I pictured the look that I knew so well, the one she always wore when she was worried, the one where a furrow would form between her brows, and then her eyes would squint and her lips would tighten.

Finally she said, "Something's better than nothing." I couldn't ignore the fear and resignation I heard in her voice. My big sister had lost her only son to lupus the year before and her loneliness was outweighing reason.

Less than a week after the call, Los Angeles was rocked by a powerful earthquake that was felt all the way to Oakland, where Joanne was living. She was home alone. A few days later she set her wedding date.

I regret that I didn't go to the wedding. My house was broken into the week before, and I wasn't comfortable leaving my two teenage daughters there alone or leaving the house unattended if they stayed with friends. Or maybe that was the excuse I told myself instead of admitting that I was afraid of flying or that I might say something to her new husband that would ruin her wedding or make her life more difficult after I left.

The day after the wedding, Tania and Ebony met me on the front porch on my way into the house after work. "You'd better sit down, Mom," Tania commanded, always the messenger. But before I could, she said, "You need to call Jayne," my cousin in San Francisco. *Why is Jayne calling?* I wondered. Mama had flown to California for Joanne's wedding. Why wasn't she the one who called? Had something happened to my mother?

The girls led me into the house, stroking my hair and my shoulders as they escorted me to the three steps that led to the kitchen, the spot where I liked to sit when I just wanted to collect myself for a moment. When she thought I was ready, Tania brought me the phone.

"Joanne's in the hospital," said Jayne. "She had a brain aneurysm. She's in a coma."

I wanted to talk to my mother. I wanted to hear her voice, to know how she was coping with this. My thoughts flew back to that August day eight years earlier in 1984, back to the night Mom called from Paris. Our beloved stepfather was in the American Hospital on the edge of life, and my oldest brother, Woody, a multilingual man who had made a career as a communications specialist in the U.S. Army—my big brother who would succumb to a heart attack eleven years later—was on his way to help her. Mom and Barney had traveled to Paris to celebrate the blessing that his cancer had gone into remission. I still have a photograph of them smiling under the marquee of Poisson et Boeuf, the restaurant where he contracted the food poisoning that would take him from us—food poisoning, not the cancer that we expected.

"Mom, how are you, Mama?" I begged when Jayne handed her the phone. "I'm fine," her standard reply for everything. But the flat, trance-like quality in her voice betrayed the numbness that I knew she was feeling. She had been the mother of the bride the day before. Was she about to end the week at her daughter's funeral? Part of me wanted to jump on the next plane, but I knew she was surrounded by our California family. They tended to ignore me when I was around them, or to somehow make me feel like I was in the way. I didn't relish being with them. Thankfully, Woody was there with Mama. I comforted myself by knowing that I was the one who would be here to give her the support she would need when she returned home.

It turned out to be a good thing that I didn't go to California. I caught a nasty flu the day after Jayne's call—the chills and fever, achy type that sends you to bed wondering if you will survive. The next afternoon while the girls were at school, I got up and slipped on my bathrobe and went downstairs to brew a cup of tea. I sat on the couch and watched whatever game show was on television, taking slow sips until the show went off, then put my cup in the sink, and started back up the stairs. When I reached the halfway point, an odd feeling came over me. At first I thought it was lightheadedness from the flu, but it felt different from that. It was something I hadn't experienced before. My body began to sway from side to side involuntarily, and I gripped the railing and hung on for dear life. When the swaying stopped, I somehow knew that my sister had reached the moment when she had to decide whether to stay or to go. The two of us had always shared a symbiotic relationship, often knowing what each other needed or wanted without sharing any words, like twins are known to do. But we were not twins; Joanne was almost two years older than I. I sensed that she was reaching out, asking me to help her with this, perhaps her final decision. I stood on the stairs for a moment wondering what to do. Then I asked her, "What do you want to do?" Soon after I made my way up the stairs and back into my bed, Woody called.

Before Mama left San Francisco, Joanne's new husband found out that she had named our mother the beneficiary on her insurance policies. She died three days after their wedding, before she was able to revise her insurance policies and name John her beneficiary. And, really, who knows whether she intended to anyway? She had changed her beneficiary from her son to our mother after she recovered from that terrible loss. Maybe she simply wasn't ready to change it again. And maybe she didn't want to leave John with anything of hers that he could abuse.

John tried to bully Mom into turning the documents over to him, a campaign he continued after she returned to Minneapolis, calling her with intimidating words and threats. But little did he know my mother was not someone who cowered under pressure. (When we were kids, we called her "the War Department.") Instead, she asked my uncle David, a lawyer, to look into John's background. We were sitting at her kitchen table having coffee when Uncle Dave called to tell her what he had learned: my sister's widower had three wives, two of whom he had never divorced and one who had died under suspicious circumstances. Not wasting any time, Mama called John and warned him that unless he wanted this information exposed, he'd better leave her alone. She never heard from him again.

INSTEAD OF TELLING CASSANDRA everything I was going through, I invited her to lunch. She had accepted and now I stood at my door, fingers glued to the doorknob. The decision to take her to lunch had been easy because our phone conversation was so warm.

I made reservations at the Rainbow Chinese restaurant, a safe place where the staff knew me. Nevertheless, I took my time getting dressed, settling on colors that would calm me: a black turtleneck, and a purple, brown, and black scarf that I hoped would draw attention away from the uncertainty I was surely wearing on my face. I laced my boots and slung my bag over my shoulder, but when I got to the door, I couldn't move. What if my friends were right? What if the kindness I'd heard in the young woman's voice on the phone was a ruse to hide the truth—that she was really about to do me in? What would I do if her lawyer was with her? What if she was wearing a wire? Was I about to walk into something I wouldn't be able to get out of? Deciding that I had been watching too many *Law and Order* episodes, I turned the doorknob and walked down the hall, hoping there would be a note on the elevator announcing that it was out of service.

Once outside, I drove slowly through the cool, misty rain that had begun to fall, stretching the twenty-minute drive to a half-hour. The soft rain fell rhythmically on my windshield like a heartbeat, seeming to echo my constant question—why am I still here?

ALL THE WAY to the restaurant, I wondered if I would recognize Cassandra. Several weeks had passed since the accident, and all I had were the memory of her rolling off the hood of my car and into the gutter, and the memory of sitting on the curb holding her head in my lap.

Once inside, I was comforted to see that my favorite bartender, Linnea, was working that day. Little did I know she would become my awesome dean at Minneapolis Community and Technical College several years later. But back then she was taking a break from academe and was holding down an hourly wage gig. Her welcoming smile left me feeling that whatever was going to happen that day, I would be all right.

The host greeted me and escorted me to the table where Cassandra was waiting. I recognized her right away. The short dark curls I had stroked while waiting for the ambulance to arrive were unmistakable, but she seemed thinner than she had appeared on the night of the accident.

We made feeble attempts at small talk while perusing the menu. Apparently, small talk wasn't one of her talents either. The weather is always a passable topic in Minnesota, so we commented on the rain. When the server brought water and took our orders, we sat in uncomfortable silence searching for words, both taking long glances at the restaurant's oversized goldfish tank and watching the lunch crowd slowly invade the popular restaurant. I ruminated briefly on another young woman named Cassandra, the character in Greek mythology who, like this girl sitting across the table from me, had curly dark hair and brown eyes. In the myth, Apollo is said to have given her the gift of prophecy but later turned it into a curse that caused all who heard her prophecies to believe she was lying. I looked around the restaurant and didn't see anyone who looked suspiciously like a lawyer, nor did Cassandra appear to be wearing a wire, so I let my guard down, but only a little. We stared at each other for a brief moment, and I was relieved to see that just as the police report had stated, she didn't seem to have endured any serious or permanent injuries from the accident.

I wanted to tell her how sorry I was for the harm I had caused her but was unable to find the words I had so carefully planned to say. Instead, she was the one who broke the silence. She cleared her throat, causing my attention to turn from the goldfish tank and my heartbeat to rise in anticipation of what I feared she was about to say. Then she looked me in the eye and said, "You are an angel."

Her voice was as clear as her sharp brown eyes. There was no mistaking what she had said, but I couldn't believe that I heard her correctly. I had been worried sick about her, and now here I was sitting across from her in this restaurant harboring a hint of a fear that she might reach into her purse and pull out a summons, or that two plainclothes detectives might walk over to us, one placing me in handcuffs while the other reads me my Miranda rights. But instead she had called me an angel.

The imaginary detectives slid out of the picture, but not before I could ask what she was thinking. "I could have killed you that night!"

She explained that she was a Mormon and had traveled here from her home state to be with a man she had fallen in love with, a guy who was in theater.

"I have always loved theater," she said. A pained yet wistful look hovered over her face when she explained that her family was conservative and straitlaced and didn't approve of her aspirations toward the arts, fearing that it might disrupt her faith.

I don't know anything about the Mormon faith but have certainly known Christians who have left family members, feeling condemned and isolated for similar reasons. Also I admit that as a parent I have experienced moments when I feared what might happen to my children if they strayed away from the belief system I tried to instill in them. I do not follow a specific faith tradition, but I do believe there is a Source higher than us who looks out for everyone, no matter their faith or their life orientations. So even though my beliefs are very different from those of her parents, I could understand their pain as well as hers.

A vague memory crossed my mind. Weren't the famous brother and sister duo Donny and Marie Osmond

Mormons? I was about to ask if her parents knew about them and their artistry, but before I could speak I saw her eyes darken and a deep sadness seemed to envelope her like a cloak.

"Things didn't work out with the guy," she said. "I don't know if he changed or if he simply wasn't what I thought he was." I watched tears begin to creep down her pale cheeks, and my thoughts returned to Cassandra of the Greek myth, the part explaining that the reason Apollo cursed her was that she went back on her promise to be his lover. "He became mean, almost cruel in the things he said to me, and after a while I lost confidence and began to feel confused."

She said that in spite of him, she enjoyed her time in Minneapolis. "I have met so many kind and wonderful people." She dried her tears with her napkin and said, "This was the first time I met people who were different from the people in my community at home. I had never seen people of different races, let alone lived next door to them or worked with them." Then after a brief pause she said, "But I miss my family and I have never stopped questioning my relationship with God."

She then looked me in the eye and said once again, "You are an angel."

She explained that until the accident she didn't think she could go back home. She feared that she would be shamed and wouldn't be allowed back into her family or her church. "The accident helped me realize that I can go home." Then she thanked me for having been willing to be the messenger that gave her that clarity.

I hugged her and walked slowly out of the restaurant, still feeling a little dazed but glad that I had followed my heart and had not allowed myself to be talked out of contacting her. I stood for a moment on the sidewalk in the misty rain, then got back into my car.

All the way home, as the rain again echoed the beats of my heart, I thought about angels—angels as messengers, angels as beings who come into our lives, some for a brief time like my siblings and my beloved stepfather, and the army of angels that I believe are always around us guiding us, the angels who led me out of my troubled marriage and let me know that I could return home, and now the angels who brought Cassandra and me together to give her the same message. Maybe that is why I am still here. Maybe my siblings completed their work here on Earth. Maybe I still have work to do.

16

STONES AND STICKS

If we can shift the paradigm then we can change the culture and the inheritance that the coming generation gets.

—Luisah Teish

There are turning points in everyone's life, though we sometimes fail to recognize them right away. I experienced one of those moments many years ago during a springtime poetry class where students were learning to make video poems.

A young woman, whom I'll call Gretel, wrote a poem about roller skating through a graveyard. Everyone in the class was intrigued by the idea, and there was plenty of nervous laughter as class members threw words like *spooky, macabre,* and *eerie* around the room as we discussed visual shots that might work well for Gretel's poem. At the end of the evening, we agreed to meet that Sunday morning at the entrance of Lakewood Cemetery, where many prominent Minnesotans are buried.

From the moment the decision was made, I felt disturbed, unable to come to grips with the thought that I might be complicit in the group's violation of the spirits of the deceased who lay peacefully in their graves. What right did we have to disturb them just because a callow young woman wanted to see herself on videotape skating through their resting place? And what about the mourners scattered throughout the cemetery? How would they feel when Gretel skated by with the rest of us walking closely behind her, gawking while they prayed for their lost loved ones or placed flowers on their graves?

THAT SUNDAY MORNING, the group followed Gretel as she skated past curved, tree-lined paths and rows of granite plaques and headstones, large statues, and imposing crypts as big as houses. Even without reading the dates, it was clear which graves had been there the longest: the older markers bore streaks of dark green, brown, or black from having been exposed to the weather for many years.

Gretel mugged for the camera, impressing us with her knowledge, naming birds that flew by and trees that were as twisted and bent as the people who lay in the graves they protected. The class members, usually quite vocal, were somber as they examined elaborate monuments and pondered the messages written on both elegant tombstones and simple markers. Susan, a tall woman with shaggy white hair and a slight limp, halted every few steps and looked around as though entranced with the scenery. I was moved when I observed Tom and Erica touch each other's hands affectionately when they slowed down to read the names of the dead and their dates of birth and death. No doubt they were contemplating a time when death might separate them.

Soon Gretel took us down a narrow pathway, which led to a thick cluster of trees bordered with pink, purple, and white flowers. She stopped and turned to face the group, then said something was in there that was really interesting. She spun around and began skating slowly down the path, glancing back to make sure we were following.

I was the first to see the lovely, weather-beaten statue of a woman who looked like she had been carved by a sculptor in the Greco-Roman era. Her figure was draped in a gown, belted at the waist, allowing her skirt to fall gently over the pedestal on which she stood. Her right hand rested serenely over her heart, and her left arm reached out in a gesture of peace. Her chiseled face was framed by long hair pulled back in a bun, and she gazed down at me with a soft smile. Her eyes, though devoid of color, appeared kind. She looked so real that it was hard to believe she was made of stone.

The class stood in a semicircle and watched Gretel's eyes take on a ghoulish sparkle. The instructor trained the camera on her, and an impish grin spread slowly over her face. The group stood waiting until finally a man with wavy blond hair and gold-rimmed glasses became impatient. "Well?" he asked. At that moment Gretel's eyes grew wide. She spun around and skated up to the statue. She lifted her arm and stuck out her finger in a gesture that reminded me of Michelangelo's *Creation of Adam* painting from the Sistine Chapel, God's finger almost touching the finger of man. Then as suddenly as she lifted her arm, she snatched it back and said, "It's a statue of a Black woman. If you touch her you'll die." Then as though propelled by a tornadic wind, she skated away, leaving petals of laughter ringing in the air along with echoes of her words.

I was paralyzed, unable to respond. My breath halted as though a knife had been jabbed into my chest and slowly twisted into my heart.

I took another look at the woman locked in that dark body made of granite, and in my mind's eye her shoulders began to slump from carrying the weight of all that stone: she seemed to almost crumble under the burden of over-work and underappreciation from cooking and cleaning for the families of Gretel's ancestors while desperately try-ing to care for her family, the families of my ancestors. At that moment I remembered every negative image I had ever heard of Black women—*oversexed, breeder, wet nurse, mammy, hostile, nappy-headed ho.* Gretel's words named something I had felt vaguely all my life but could not describe with words of my own. The cautionary warn-ings from our mothers and grandmothers: "You gotta work harder and be better if you want to be seen as just as good as white girls"; "You gotta go through a lot of pain to be beautiful" (translation: keep your hair straightened and your butt looking flatter); Billie Holiday's lyrics, "Southern trees bear strange fruit . . . black bodies hanging from the poplar tree"; the blue eyes that Toni Morrison's charac-ter Pecola prayed for, believing that they would stop the abuse she was suffering, stop her from being seen as "dirt"; the horrific story of the Hottentot Venus, the orphaned eighteenth-century South African woman whose large but-tocks and extended labia caused her Dutch enslavers to turn her into a sideshow attraction; the degrading ways we Black women are depicted in movies or shaking our asses in hip-hop videos; the ways we are devalued in school and the workplace; how our men who reject us and men of other races, who look past us or leer at us with hidden lust. All of those images and more came crashing into my heart. Gretel's words made it clear that in the eyes of the world the Black woman is poison: "If you touch her you'll die."

I can't lay all of the blame on Gretel. Nor can I blame the group's nonreaction entirely on them. No doubt, Gretel was repeating what she'd heard all of her life. No doubt, her comment was unremarkable to the others in the group for the same reason. Throughout history, the Black woman has had to struggle with the perception that her Blackness makes her as venomous as a sting from the tongue of a poisonous asp or the bite of a black widow spider. In chapter one of the biblical *Song of Solomon,* one of the most beautiful love poems ever written, King Solomon's Shulamite bride has the misfortune of having to implore the daughters of Jerusalem not to look down on her. She says in defense of herself, "I am black but comely."

Unfortunately, we are still struggling with this perception. On June 27, 2008, the *Atlanta Journal–Constitution* reported that Chiman Rai, a retired math professor, was sentenced to life in prison for having paid a hit man $10,000 to murder his son's African American wife. A native of India, Rai feared that the marriage would cast a stigma on his family, explaining with no remorse that India's rigid caste system deems Blacks the lowest caste, and Black women the absolute lowest, since women are believed to be lower than men in his culture.

I HAVE THREE BEAUTIFUL, intelligent daughters. I have had to help them maintain their self-images over and over again, even as I've attempted to heal my own. I also fully understand the horror of what is happening to our young men. I have a son who was incarcerated for ten years in the federal penitentiary. But there seems to be a conspiracy of silence around our girls and women. Could it be that in large part our incarceration is invisible? That we are locked up in our bodies?

Like countless Black mothers, I have worked hard to train my daughters to be proud of who they are in a world that would have them be ashamed of their darkness. For Black women, loving ourselves and passing that self-love down to our daughters and our granddaughters is a difficult task. Centuries of negation often makes us feel like we need to adopt a hard, protective shell, which is either praised as strength or dismissed as hostility. In short, we turn ourselves into stone.

I LEFT THE CEMETERY wondering what it would take to liberate us. Today, as I think about what my parents had to go through—much that I didn't learn about until after they had passed on—and the stories my students are carrying, I worry. As I see my grandchildren move through a world where the current president has given the green light to white supremacy following President Barack Obama's eight years of hope, where Black and Brown people are under violent attack, I have to ask: What is it that will set us free?

ACKNOWLEDGMENTS

Thanks first to the folks at the University of Minnesota Press for believing in this work. Special thanks to my amazing editor, Erik Anderson, for shepherding me and my book through the editorial process and for putting up with my whining. Thanks also to Louisa Castner for your sensitive copyediting.

To *Water~Stone Review,* the Minnesota Historical Society Press, *Black Renaissance Noire,* Stylus Press, Erlbaum Press, Seven Stories Press, and Spout Press, and to editors John Colburn, Julie Landsman, Mary F. Rockcastle, Meri Nana-Ama Danquah, Sun Yung Shin, Alexs D. Pate, Pamela Fletcher, Quincy Troupe, Sandra Tutwiler, Eugene B. Redmond, Ann Regan, and posthumously to J. Otis Powell—many thanks to all of you for publishing versions of some of the essays in this book.

Thank you to the Minnesota State Arts Board for giving me the gift of time to complete my manuscript, and to Paulette Bates Alden, Barrie Jean Borich, and Patricia Weaver Francisco for your feedback along the way. Special thanks to Scott Edelstein for your multileveled consultations.

To Karyn Sproles, who knew I was a teacher before I knew it; to Alice Moorhead, Veena Deo, everyone in Hamline University's English department, and to Linnea

Stenson at Minneapolis Community and Technical College, for your encouragement throughout my teaching journey; to friends and mentors Andrea "Andy" Gilats and Julie Landsman; and to my students, who continue to teach me so much.

Huge thanks to Neal Cuthbert, Cynthia Gehrig, Nancy Fushan, Mary Pickard, and Claire Chang, for your loving and consistent support of my work in the community through the Jerome, McKnight, Bush, St. Paul, and St. Paul Travelers Foundations; and to Diane Espaldon, Shannon Kennedy, and Leslie Wolfe for working with me through the transition and merger. Special thanks to Julie Bates-McGillis for growing SASE's programs at Intermedia Arts and to everyone who helped make SASE happen, especially Brandon Lussier and Sandy Moore.

To the women in my writing groups: Sherrie Fernandez-Williams, Mary Moore Easter, Carla-Elaine Johnson, Kyoko Katayama, Joan Maze, Mai Neng Moua, Nora Murphy, Marcie Rendon, Sagirah Shahid, Jna Shelomith, Buffy Smith, Joan Trygg. Special thanks to my bestest writing buddy and writing doula, Diane Wilson.

And, finally, thanks and reverence to Mom, Dad, Barney—I miss you. To my amazing children—Stevie, Julian, Iris, Tania, and Ebony. To my grandchildren—Trent, Xaundra, Keenan, Tess, Marselais, Jordyn, Nia, and Najah. To my great-granddaughter, Penny, and those yet to come into the world.

PUBLICATION HISTORY

"Liza" (Prologue) and "Earth Angels" were published as a chapbook by Spout Press in 2019.

"Coming Clean" was originally published in *The Poverty and Education Reader: A Call for Equity in Many Voices,* ed. Julie Landsman and Paul Gorski (Stylus Press, 2013), 223–29.

"Tania's Birthday" was originally published as "Natalie's Birthday" in *Water~Stone Review* 4 (St. Paul: Hamline University, 2001).

"Expectations and Assumptions" was originally published as "Low Expectations Are the Worst Form of Racism" in *White Teachers/Diverse Classrooms,* second edition, ed. Julie Landsman and Chance W. Lewis (Sterling, Va.: Stylus Publishing, 2011), 243–54.

A version of "I Want to Know My Name" became a song composed by Joan Griffith and Janis Hardy and published by Pleasing Dog Music. The song was commissioned by the Twin Cities Women's Choir and performed on February 7, 2004, in "Stitching the World, Weaving Our Song: A Patchwork of African American Voices."

Previous versions of "The Bank Robbery" were published in *Blues Vision: African American Writing from Minnesota,* ed. Alexs D. Pate, Pamela Fletcher, and J. Otis Powell (St. Paul: Minnesota Historical Society Press, 2015), 141–47; and in *Black Renaissance Noire* (New York: New York University, 2010).

Previous versions of "Neighborhood Watch" were published in Sandra J. Winn Tutwiler, *Teachers as Collaborative Partners: Working with Diverse Families and Communities* (Lawrence Erlbaum Associates, 2005), 95; and as "'Coffee': Words from Minneapolis–St. Paul," *Drumvoices Revue* 9 (Edwardsville, Ill.: Southern Illinois University, 2000), 117–19.

"My Daughter, Myself" was originally published under the author pseudonym Rasheeda, in *Colors* (November/December 1993).

"Say What?" was originally published in *A Good Time for the Truth: Race in Minnesota,* ed. Sun Yung Shin (St. Paul: Minnesota Historical Society Press, 2016), 99–108.

Previous versions of "Stones and Sticks" were published in *Blues Vision: African American Writing from Minnesota,* ed. Alexs D. Pate, Pamela Fletcher, and J. Otis Powell (St. Paul: Minnesota Historical Society Press, 2015), 205–8; and in *The Black Body,* ed. Meri Nana-Ama Danquah (New York: Seven Stories Press, 2009), 167–74.